THE FOOD THAT HELD THE WORLD TOGETHER

We owe a debt of
gratitude
to the Greatest Generation—
that we can never repay—

Cleo Lampos

Also by Gail Kittleson

In Times Like These
With Each New Dawn
A Purpose True
All for the Cause
Until Then
Kiss Me Once Again
In This Together
Catching Up With Daylight

Also by Cleo Lampos

A Mother's Song
Dust Between the Stitches
Riding the Rails to Home
Piecing Fabrics~Mending Lives

THE
Food
that Held
THE World Together

Gail Kittleson & Cleo Lampos

WordCrafts

Contents

Acknowledgements

The authors appreciate Sherri Wilson Johnson's expertise in the completion of this book. Her technical expertise and organizational skills proved invaluable to the project. Special thanks to the family of Dorothy Woebbeking for the use of personal photographs.

We extend a debt of gratitude to the veterans who left behind their written testimonies, and the people still living who shared from their cache of memories, recipes and stories that have given the personal touch to this historical book. While we have endeavored to contact all individuals portrayed in these stories, or their surviving family members, some have been lost to history. In these cases it is our sincere desire to be respectful of their sacrifices and to honor their memories.

Introduction

World War II—how does one even begin to grasp the scope of this many-faceted era?

The impossibility of this task requires us to focus on one area at a time. In researching a fiction story, this is what authors do, and each plunge into the history reaps new insights to be woven into the tale's fabric.

For example, one of Gail's readers quipped, "Your novels all include characters growing something and cooking or baking." She hadn't really thought of it that way, but since food was so vital during this era, it makes sense.

Because of wartime rationing, World War II folks faced fresh challenges to feed their families. The thought of running out of food or not being able to make ends meet led to great effort—many of these citizens had not so long ago survived the hunger of the Great Depression.

Many stories from this period revolve around food, and reading them motivated us to further explore this topic. In the process, so many questions occurred. Most of us are familiar with victory gardens, but what more do they have to teach us? How did soldiers cope with their hunger on foreign soil?

How did the food industry respond to wartime needs? What innovations developed as families sought ways to show their soldiers their love and concern? We found answers to many of our questions through speaking with people with treasured memories of this era and in the wealth of available information about this period.

A huge thank-you from both of us to everyone who shared personal stories. Thank you for "Putting on your thinking caps and letting the memories flow."

We all experience life through visual, aural, olfactory, tactile, and gustatory senses—we see, hear, smell, touch, and taste as we journey through our days. During the deprivations of war, taste and smell became supremely important. One whiff or bit of flavor could bring *home* back to a soldier or nurse deployed far away from loved ones.

We hope you relish these stories and facts as much as we enjoyed discovering them!

Cleo and Gail

The Home Front

Chapter 1

"The Coffee Pot Is On"

Maybe the code phrase lacked the clandestine allure that wartime secrecy dictated. Everyone knew that "loose lips sink ships." But these words sped through the local grapevine in the hush-hush tones that signaled a covert operation. Hundreds of people responded by switching to high gear and silent passage.

"The coffee pot is on." A Union Pacific troop train was headed for Nebraska, a point of destination for a ten to fifteen minute stop in order to top off water levels in the steam engine tanks and re-lubricate the wheels. The depot's canteen operated from Christmas Day, 1941, to April 1, 1946.

Many trains pulled into the North Platte station from five a.m. to well after midnight. Local citizens met the uniformed men—these were people who had "put the coffee pot on."

"The coffee pot is on." Originally, these code words signaled the city to show up at the platform to encourage the men of the Nebraska National Guard's 134th Infantry Regiment. These soldiers were the sons of local farmers and businessmen. But this time, the crowd cheered a surprised group of 300 trained recruits traveling to assignments overseas.

Somebody else's sons. But the North Platte folks greeted these Kansas boys with cigarettes, candy, smiles, tears, and laughter. Thus, the idea of meeting every troop train with a canteen was born. When the war ended, six million GIs had enjoyed this heart-filling break from the unknown.

"The coffee pot is on." Initially, volunteers needed to prepare food for the canteen drew from a remote plains community of 12,000 persons. Women who knew how to cook, bake, and serve devoted themselves to this work. The daily shopping list bought by private citizens included at least "175 loaves of bread, 100 pounds of meat, 13 pounds of cheese, 2 quarts of peanut butter, 45 pounds of coffee, 40 quarts of cream, and 25 dozens of rolls."[1]

The myriad dozens of cookies and donuts, as well as homemade cakes, were created by farm women who knew how to make their ration cards stretch. Fried chicken, beef sandwiches, and ham slices joined garden vegetables from surrounding farms. Local citizens preserved pickles and applesauce to be used for the troops, and in season, the women served wild pheasant hunted by their husbands.

Older men drove cars laden with food and fueled by their own ration cards. Then they loaded and unloaded the treats for GIs whose young faces tore at their hearts. David Vail, an agricultural historian for the University of Nebraska at Kearney observed: "Farmers viewed themselves as part of fighting the war by producing food for troops overseas."

The Canteen was supported by 125 towns which sent 55,000 volunteers to help feed the troops at home as well.

"The coffee pot is on." This encrypted message brought a bevy of "platform girls." These teenagers carried baskets of fruit, matches, and candy bars to greet the young men and guide them to tables in the station heaving with sandwiches, hard boiled eggs, and other tasty home-cooked vittles.

The hospital trains held men who were unable to disembark. The older women went aboard so their daughters would be spared the bandages and suffering. Walking among the wounded, they handed out food as well as decks of cards, reading materials, and good wishes. They kept their smiles fixed and their comments positive as thoughts of husbands and sons already overseas threatened to put tears on their cheeks.

All the glass and metal containers were returned on the next train heading back to North Platte, and volunteers washed dishes by hand to be ready for the next day.

"The coffee pot is on." These signal words brought a gleam to music lovers' eyes. The Canteen boasted both a jukebox and a piano. Sometimes a lone soldier or sailor tickled the ivories, and this musical interlude helped to keep them emotionally stable.

Those who would rather dance than eat found willing partners in the teenage girls who enjoyed "In the Mood," "Tuxedo Junction," or any tune with a cheery message. A great deal of music exploded in the room during the fifteen-minute respite.

"The coffee pot is on." Popcorn balls gave variety to the treats, and molasses served to sweeten the popcorn in place of rationed sugar and corn syrup. And, for the Tyron Ladies, the fun of putting the names and addresses of high school age girls in their tiny town into popcorn balls proved to be a friendly activity.

Get a pen pal and keep the boys from getting lonesome.

Ethel's name and address ended up in one of the treats given to a young soldier named Virgil Butolph. Ethel and Virgil wrote and exchanged pictures for several years. After the war, they married, had five children, and enjoyed thirty-two years together.

All because the Canteen sent out popcorn balls.

"The coffee pot is on." These words pressed some into action,

and others into a work of the spirit. Helen Johnson helped feed 2,000 brave souls a day. She watched the young soldiers hurry from eating at the Canteen and load up onto the hard wooden seats of the trains. From a heart of concern, she did the only thing that she thought would give them light on a journey into the darkest of tunnels.

"I would pray. For all of them. I would watch them get onto the train, and I would ask the Lord to bless and keep them. I wanted to keep smiling, in case they turned around to look at us when they left. But I was praying for them, with my eyes open."[2]

"The coffee pot is on." The love and appreciation that the soldiers and sailors experienced through food carried them through tough times ahead. Russ Fay expressed what most GIs felt.

"I can still taste it. I would say that a majority of the men on the battlefields knew exactly what North Platte was… They would talk about it like it was a dream. Out of nowhere: 'How'd you like to have some of that food from the North Platte Canteen right about now?"[3]

"The coffee pot is on." Train loads of troops about to be deployed to parts unknown experienced unconditional support, respect, and love through the homemade sandwiches, cakes, cookies, and fruit grown and prepared by frugal Midwestern farming families.

The depth of the experience changed so many lives. The war was fought on the home front with busy hands, patriotic hearts, and tables of food that provided a lingering taste of home.

"The coffee pot is still on" in our nation's collective memory.

BEEF SALAD SANDWICHES
From the North Platte Canteen Cookbook
published by *Lincoln County Historical Museum*

Ingredients
    Roast beef, ground up
    Pickle relish
    Homemade mayonnaise

Combine roast beef, pickle relish, and homemade mayonnaise and put on two slices of bread.

HOMEMADE MAYONNAISE

Ingredients
    2 eggs
    ½ cup sugar
    ½ teaspoon salt
    ½ cup vinegar
    1 cup water
    1 tablespoon flour
    1 teaspoon mustard powder
    Cream or Miracle Whip

Combine all ingredients and cook over a double boiler until thick. Cool. Add cream or Miracle Whip until right consistency.

"North Platte hasn't any big war industries. I guess you could say we've started our own—exporting morale."

Reader's Digest, April, 1944

Chapter 2

Jell-O: The Sweet Treat

How does the home front support the troops overseas? With Jell-O.

While war raged on far-away continents, many a cook focused on devising a culinary display rather than letting despair win the battle of the mind and heart. Every home-maker in the 1940's owned at least one tin Jell-O mold to give her jiggly creation a presence on the table.

The tuna salad shone in gelatin shaped like a fish. Cherry flavored Jell-O filled with fresh fruit was spooned from a molded ring. Marshmallows and nuts added interest to lime desserts. Even bits of celery, cucumbers, carrots and nuts filled a high crowned mold on a plate. From cooked spinach to chicken salad, housewives stretched leftovers and scraps of food by encasing them in wiggly gelatin.

It was easy to prepare Jell-O because the main ingredient came in a small box, saving preparation time. A Red Crest Salad consisted of strawberry Jell-O with chopped tomatoes and pickles stirred in for a colorful display. The fact that the package contained sugar meant that the family's sugar ration card was not used up so quickly. Jell-O: economical, efficient, and delicious.

"As World War II began, Jell-O molds were a way to 'prove to you and your friends that you can still do luscious entertaining in spite of shortages and rations."[1] A favorite wartime recipe called "Olive Relish" boasted olives, pickles, celery and vinegar set into green lime Jell-O.

Jell-O created a mess-free salad. Unlike the green leafy salads served in large bowls and spilling over the sides with oily dressing, jellied salads were never tossed. They stayed within the borders of the plate.

This molded treat avoided the untidiness of conventional greens by holding them intact within gelatin. In an era when the world seemed chaotic and disjointed, a culinary delight on the table that actually had shape and substance may have subconsciously held emotions in check.

Jell-O followed the Japanese Americans forced to leave their homes for internment camps. Mary Tsukamoto tells how she decided what to pack. "I started to gather small sacks of rice and…packages of dehydrated soup and Jell-O and things that were light, so that they wouldn't be such a heavy baggage for us to carry because they said you could only take what you could carry. And we knew we had to take blankets, sheets, bedding, and clothes." Undoubtedly, eating the Jell-O would constitute an exceptional treat in the internment camp.

For the Rosie the Riveter set, making a bowl of gelatin with finely chopped cabbage, celery and red pepper for dinner demonstrated care and love to their families. Cost effective, convenient, nutritious and versatile, Jell-O won the hearts of women who needed time to roll bandages for the Red Cross, work in a defense plant, or grow vegetables in community Victory Gardens.

The home front prided itself on its ability to sacrifice for the men overseas. One might say that America's support of the troops began at the dinner table with Jell-O.

The Difference between Gelatin and Jell-O

Gelatin is a colorless and tasteless water-soluble protein prepared from collagen extracted from the bones, skin and connective tissues of animals. Gelatin may be used in pharmaceutical or cosmetic industries as well as the food industry.

Jell-O is a brand name for sweet and fruity flavored gelatin. It is a mix of artificial flavors and food colors added to gelatin. Easy to use, the cook simply dissolves the mixture in hot water, stirs, and adds cold water.

Jell-O is strictly utilized as food. Because it uses gelatin derived from animal bones and skin, Jell-O is not considered vegetarian or vegan. High in sugar (18 grams per serving), and low in fiber and protein, Jell-O provides instant energy but little nutritional value. Gelatin contains collagen, which aids in bone health, preventing joint pain and the aging of skin.

RECIPE FOR GARDEN SALAD RING

Ingredients
    1 package Lemon Jell-O
    1 cup hot water
    1 cup cold water
    ¾ cup shredded cabbage
    1 tablespoon minced chives
    2 tablespoon vinegar
    ¼ teaspoon salt
    1 hard-cooked egg, sliced
    2 tablespoons thinly sliced radishes

Dissolve Jell-O in hot water. Add cold water, chill until slightly thickened. Meanwhile, marinate cabbage and chives in vinegar and salt for ½ hour. Place ¼ cup of Jell-O in mold. In this arrange egg slices and chill until firm. Fold marinated vegetables and radishes into Jell-O and turn onto firm layer. Chill all until firm. Unmold. Makes 4 servings. When the salad is unmolded, the sliced eggs lie on the top, while the vegetables add color and interest to the Jell-O ring.

"KNOX helps stretch rationed foods into delicious, nourishing dishes your family will thoroughly enjoy."
Knox Wartime Recipes, published 1943.

Chapter 3

SPAM: Home in a Can

I n the middle of the Great Depression, Hormel Foods Corporation needed a product to stand out in the meat business, something that would transcend seasonal changes experienced with fresh meat. The answer for plant-manager Jay Hormel lay in developing canned meat.

By the end of the Great Depression, he introduced pork shoulder, an under-utilized cut of meat, vacuum packed in a can. Later, ham was combined with the mix. Each can contained pork shoulder meat with ham, salt, water, sugar and sodium nitrite.

In a naming contest at a New Year's Eve party, Actor Kenneth Daigneau coined the term SPAM. Some claim that it means "spiced ham," while others suggest it is an acronym for "shoulder and pork ham."

The name stuck, and on May 11, 1937 the trademark was registered. Housewives started to buy this meat that did not need refrigeration and leant to a variety of culinary delights. Homemakers liked the ingenuity and resourcefulness of the product. In 1940, a twenty page recipe-book featured 50 ways to use a can of SPAM.

The tins rolled off the conveyor belt just in time for WWII in 1941. Allied and American troops needed tasty, easy-to-use rations. Fresh meat was difficult to transport to the front, so cans of SPAM provided a safe protein source for breakfast, lunch and dinner.

George "Joe" Richner, a navigator in the 8th Army Air Force in 1944-45, says, "We were forced to land in France. There was a problem with fuel. I remember eating canned meat. It was part of the survival kit we were issued. We ate it right out of the can."[1]

Even Dwight D. Eisenhower chowed down on the gelatinous meat. "During WWII, of course, I ate my share of SPAM along with the millions of other soldiers. I'll even confess to a few unkind remarks about it- uttered during the strain of battle, you understand. But as Commander in Chief, I believe I can still officially forgive you (Hormel) for your only sin: sending so much of it to us."[2]

Every week during the war, the military purchased over 15 million cans of SPAM. The long lasting meat was served in Guam, Hawaii, Okinawa, the Philippines and other Pacific Islands, and the natives incorporated it into their diets.

England declared the tinned meat as a "wartime delicacy." Margaret Thatcher ate it on Boxing Day in 1943. "We had friends in and opened a tin of SPAM luncheon meat. We had some lettuce and tomatoes and peaches, so it was SPAM and salad."[3]

Quite proper.

SPAM was consumed by soldiers on the beaches, in the woods, on tanks, and under fire—right from the can. But if time permitted, SPAM proved delicious when prepared with rice or accompanying a sunny-side up egg for breakfast.

Between two slices of bread and doused with Tabasco sauce, the product made a great sandwich. Kabobs with pineapple grilled over a fire became popular in the tropical war zones. Cubed-up SPAM mixed into freeze-dried K and B rations satisfied many a soldier's hunger.

At 310 calories for a one hundred gram serving, SPAM delivered a lot of nutrition to bolster the energy of military personnel. However, "Uncle Spam," as GIs called the meat, was not only eaten. This handy product served to grease guns, the cans were used for scrap metal and soldiers used it to barter for other items.

SPAM was: "the last line of defense between battle-weary soldiers and starvation," according to Hormel. If an army marches on its stomach, then the US military moved on SPAM.

Thank you, Jay Hormel, for developing a food fit for a nation at war.

Note: SPAM also affected civilians under duress in occupied territory. For example, in France, Jean Jacques Tay of Strawberry, AZ, tells how as a child, he and his family watched the Allies driving north through the foothills of the Alps.

In Jean Jacques' small village and others along the way, the troops were met by civilians offering fresh tomatoes, grapes, and other produce in exchange for Hershey candy bars and—you guessed it—cans of SPAM.

Jean Jacques, now 82, states, "I still love eating SPAM!"

SPAM SANDWICHES

From the collection of family recipes of Ina Meiners
Webster City, Iowa

Although the meat can be eaten cold or hot, Ina claims that Spam sandwiches are best when fried in a skillet that gives the meat a crisp finish.

Pour 1-2 tablespoons of oil into a skillet and heat oil. Add a drizzle of maple syrup to take away some of the saltiness of the Spam.

Remove the spam intact from the can and slice into one inch strips.

Fry for 2-3 minutes on one side, then flip onto the other side for 1-2 minutes.

Place on sandwich bread or a bun. Add condiments to taste.

"Accept the challenges so that you can feel the exhilaration of victory."

George S. Patton

Chapter 4

Potatoes: The Spud's Your Bud

How does a nation feed its people with nutritious food? After the great Depression, the US Department of Food Administration gave the potato a boost. Having lived through dire times when homemakers learned to make meals out of whatever was on hand, the launch to promote potatoes agreed with the creativity of these cooks.

They fried potatoes to accompany eggs or toast at breakfast. Potato soup for lunch filled stomachs. Scalloped potatoes in the evening used up scraps of ham and bits of cheese. One winter comfort food that frugal housewives invented was

the Cheese, Onion and Potato Pie, which supplied layers of spud goodness.

Women mixed kielbasa, sauerkraut and potato into a stew. They made mashed potatoes, baked spuds, potato salad, or beef stew. Thick or thin, string or cube, potatoes graced the tables of WWII home front families at least twice a day.

The British especially embraced the potato as a source of Vitamin C, B1, B6, Folate, Iron, Magnesium, and Potassium. The high yield of 3 to 5 pounds of produce per seed potato provides a bountiful harvest.

Planted in the *Dig for Victory* gardens, the homegrown tubers helped to save the fleet, as there was no need to ship them from overseas. Food mileage began to be measured in yards and feet, and as green spaces across Britain turned into vegetable patches, the *Dig for Victory* campaign introduced Potato Pete.

His role in the war entailed bringing enthusiasm to the cooking and consumption of potatoes. Dr. Carrot was

invented as a mate for Potato Pete, who encouraged eating vegetables. There was a weekly prize for the greengrocer with the best vegetable display.

Potato Pete also gave his advice on the radio and in a recipe book.

He sang,

> *Potatoes new. Potatoes old*
> *Potatoes in a salad cold...*
> *Enjoy them all including chips*
> *Remembering spuds don't come in ships.*[1]

The Ministry of Food used Potato Pete's antics to help alleviate the tensions of a nation coping with the challenges of rationing. The resulting recipes became legendary.

As American troops assembled to head overseas, the U.S. Army Quartermaster Corps panicked. Colonel Logan needed a food that was lightweight, nutritious, and had a long shelf life. Logan contacted the J.R. Simplot Company.

As it happened, Simplot had been toying with a method to dehydrate potatoes and onions, and his process was perfected just in time. During the war years, the company shipped thirty-three million pounds of dehydrated potatoes and five million pounds of dried onions per year to the military.

This amounted to one-third of what was needed. "I think we delivered a lot of potatoes during the year, and we learned a lot in Idaho because of it," Simplot stated.

Potatoes also served in a combat mission. On April 5, 1943,

I make a good Soup!

Says **POTATO PETE**

the Fletcher class ship *USS O'Bannon* was returning to Maine from the Pacific Theatre. The enemy sub known as RO-34 came into its sights. The sub moved along on the surface as its crew dozed. *O'Bannon's* skipper decided to ram the sub, but through error, found itself alongside the enemy instead—too close to use weapons or even sidearms.

The Japanese scrambled for their deck guns, so the GIs needed to keep them away from the weapons. Bins of potatoes on deck held the answer. The American sailors threw them with might, and the half-asleep enemy thought that the thuds of the spuds rose from hand grenades.

The potato war gave the O'Bannon time to gain distance and recalibrate, and then the sailors took care of the sub. The crew was awarded a plaque from the Association of Maine Potato Growers.

Reliance on potatoes for a quick meal that fills the tummy is still a mainstay of American culture. So many recipes date back to the homemakers of WWII, and Americans still believe a spud is worth planting in the garden.

CHEESE AND POTATO DUMPLINGS

Ingredients

2 pounds of peeled potatoes (set aside the peel to bake in the oven for another delicious snack)

2 reconstituted dried eggs (or 2 fresh)

3 to 4 ounces strong grated cheese

Salt and pepper

Dried herbs such as thyme

Method

Cook potatoes in boiling salted water.

Set aside to drain in colander for ten minutes.

Mash potatoes, return to saucepan over low heat, add seasoning and herbs. Mix well.

Add eggs and half the cheese, mix well again and stir until potatoes firm up.

Once cooled a little, form into 10 balls and roll in remaining grated cheese.

Place on greased baking tray and bake in hot oven for 20 minutes or so until brown and crusty.[2]

"His weapon may be a plough, a milk pail, an axe—but every farmer is in the front line of America's defense today."

A 1942 advertisement from *Farm Journal*

Chapter 5

Organ Meats: Learn to Love

In 1952, the effects of wartime food education lingered in the classroom of Sherman No. 7, my one-room country school near Manson, Iowa. There at my desk during lunch, I had my first taste of tongue sandwiches. On store bought bread.

Gladly, I handed over my sandwich of peanut butter and homemade strawberry jam on slices of home-baked bread from my lunch box. The trade complete. I savored this delicious delicacy created from an organ meat.

During World War II, the United States needed meat for our soldiers and allies. As people ate less meat stateside, the government feared widespread protein deficiencies. The men in Washington wanted the home front to switch from cooking standard cuts of meat to eating kidneys, brains, hearts, stomachs, intestines and other "organ meats."

But organ meats did not rate high on the social ladder—they were associated with people in rural areas with clodhopper manners. The government realized it would be a hard sell to move thousands of pounds of organ meats to the general population so the troops could have choice cuts of pork and beef. Without surveying the GIs, those in charge of feeding soldiers and sailors knew that complaints galore would result if heart, liver and other plentiful organ meats appeared in mess halls.

So the government presented a question to the public: "Why don't you eat organ meats in the first place?" A campaign designed to convince adults to taste and learn to cook unfamiliar meat was launched. "The first thing they did was say, 'Let's have a much smaller ask. Let's ask people to occasionally try an organ meat. Insert organ meat into your meal planning. Just try it for variety.'"[1]

The *"variety meats"* that the butchers sold for fewer ration points included tripe, kidneys, tongue, heart, and liver. The change in attitude towards these meats was partially due to the efforts of community groups' "variety" cooking classes. The chefs explained how to work around the odor, texture and appearance of these unfamiliar meats.

Recipes and discussion followed. As the population tried out the recipes, the food tasted more palatable. Best of all, the cheaper cuts left more ration points for a desired dish. Stuffed heart one night, but maybe a steak on the weekend.

Even the White House included thrifty meals, due to

Eleanor Roosevelt's leading. The President complained in a note to his wife, "I have been getting sweetbreads about six times a week." Eleanor showed him all the ways sweetbreads could be prepared: broiled, roasted, creamed or on toast.

Sweetbreads come from the thymus gland and pancreas. Other nutrient laden organ meats such as kidneys, liver and brains became staples on the President's table.[2]

My mother told stories about frying eggs and brains for my father before he went to work. Those were "the war years" and liver braised with bacon and onions graced our table many times.

Today, we eat organ meats every day without comment. Braunschweiger is a smoked sausage made from liver and onion powder, and tastes delicious on crackers. Liverwurst is cooked and seasoned differently, but still tasty. Headcheese is made from the heart, tongue, and other parts of an animal's head, a delicacy for sure.

What started as a patriotic duty to serve variety meats to our families morphed into a way of eating that expanded into the next decade. Housewives discovered a new perspective by exchanging recipes, discussing results, and enjoying an economical choice to high meat prices. They learned that variety meat was something that "people like us eat."

In 1971, my husband and I bought our first half of beef from a butcher to pack our newly purchased freezer. The butcher inquired: Did I want the heart for stuffing or did I want it ground into the hamburger? I chose the latter.

During WWII, cooking creatively and frugally with organ meats became a patriotic act enjoyed in the kitchen. Those who savor variety meats even today benefited from their action.

STUFFED HEART

Wash heart well, removing veins, arteries and clotted blood.

Stuff with a dressing made from one cup breadcrumbs, three tablespoons corn oil, small onion, sage and parsley.

Brown the heart in a small amount of fat in a fireless cooker vessel.

Be sure it is browned on all sides.

Add a cup and a half of hot water, a bay leaf, two cloves and a fourth teaspoon of peppercorns.

Heat to boiling and place in fireless cooker with well-heated stone. Leave for three to four hours.

Just before serving, lift from the liquor and brown in oven. Thicken the stock and use as gravy.[3]

"Healthy citizens are the greatest asset any country can have."

Winston Churchill

Chapter 6

Eggs: The All-Around Staple

In England, fresh eggs were rationed in June 1942. As a result, the government developed dried egg powder from the United States to supplement the egg allowance.

A tin equaled a dozen eggs and was "extra to your regular egg ration." The populace was unreceptive to the idea, boosted by a poster created by the Ministry of Food.

"Dried eggs are the complete hen's eggs, both the white and the yolk, dried to a powder. Nothing is added. Nothing but the moisture and the shell taken away, leaving the eggs themselves as wholesome, as digestible and as full of nourishment and health-promoting value as if you had just taken the eggs new laid from the nest. So put the eggs back into your breakfast menus. And what about a big, creamy omelette for supper? You can have it savoury, or sweet, now that you get extra jam.

In wartime the most difficult food for us to get are the body-builders. Dried eggs build muscles and repair tissue in just the same way as do chops and steaks; and are better for health protection. So we are particularly lucky to be able to get dried egg to make for any shortage of other body-builders such as meat, fish, cheese and milk.

Your allowance of dried egg is equal to three eggs a week. You can now get one 12-egg pack per four-week rationing period. Children, holders of green ration books, get two-packets per rationing period. You can buy dried eggs at the shop you are registered for shell eggs; poultry keepers can buy anywhere.

Don't hoard your dried eggs; use them up! There are plenty more coming.

Note: Do not make up dried eggs until you are ready to use them. They should not be allowed to stand after they have been mixed with water or other liquid. Use dry when making cakes and so on, and add a little more moisture when mixing.

Free – Dried egg leaflet containing many interesting recipes will be sent on receipt of a postcard addressed to Dept. 627E, Food Advice Service, Ministry of Food, London W1."

The Ministry of Food even pushed dried eggs on their posters for fresh fruit and vegetables with the information that "all the rich goodness and the flavour of fresh eggs remains. Mix with water as directed on the tin and use just as you would use a freshly beaten egg."

Leaflet Number eleven from the British Ministry of Food focused on utilizing dried eggs in various recipes: Yorkshire pudding, bacon and egg pie, egg cutlets, scrambled eggs and egg in a nest. These dishes found their way across the ocean to the States by letter or word of mouth—here is how one makes:

EGG IN A NEST

Beat the egg. Cut holes from the centre of each slice of bread with small scone cutter.

Dip the slices quickly into water and then fry on one side (in dripping if you have any available) until golden brown.

Turn on to the other side, pour half the egg into the hole in each slice of bread, cook till the bread is brown on the underneath side.

The bread cut from the centres can be fried and served with the slices. Serve straight away with salt and pepper to season and some HP or Daddies sauce or brown Chop sauce.

Speaking of eggs, Eleanor Roosevelt scrambled some every Sunday night in a chafing dish right at the dining table. After her husband first took office, she published a book called, *It's up to the Women*.

"The mother of a family should look upon her housekeeping and the planning of meals as a scientific occupation," she wrote. Her section on food appeared in the chapter called "Family Health," and opened with this advice: "Do not eat too much."

Eleanor, who grew up relying on servants and governesses, adopted the educational "home economics" attitude toward homemaking. This was one presidency not known for lavish lunches and dinners, and all across the nation, women followed suit.

Making do in the kitchen was nothing new—many World War II women had grown up during the Depression. Instead of using fresh oats, for example, a muffin recipe might incorporate leftover breakfast porridge. The egg might be mixed from powder, sugar would be added by teaspoons instead of third or half cups, and a tablespoon of shortening would suffice. Focusing on economy, the recipe might produce only six muffins.

Women who were reared on Vinegar Pie, in which a mixture of flour, nutmeg, butter, vinegar and hot water substituted for fruit filling, already knew how to scrimp and save.

Meanwhile, the lowly egg became symbolic of hearth and home for American GIs stationed far away. They would pay exorbitant prices for real eggs and often make great efforts to find them.

Philip T. Rutherford, in *On arms and eggs: GI mania on the battlefields of WWII*, writes, "... the widespread passion for fresh whole eggs was both a reflection of their scarcity in government-issued rations and a reaction against the loathsome dehydrated egg products force-fed to American soldiers throughout the war. It also demonstrates that GIs found fresh eggs both physically and psychologically comforting. Filling, easy to cook, easy to digest, usually eaten hot, fresh eggs were a high-protein alternative to the canned hash, pork and beans, soapy cheese, and dismal SPAM ubiquitous in American field rations, and one cherished by frontline troops across the theaters of war...To the GIs on the warfront, fresh eggs embodied the safety and security of faraway civilian life..."

After parachuting into the Netherlands in Operation Market Garden, one soldier reveals how precious eggs had become to him and his buddies. He said the Dutch treated them as heroes and told how one trooper found some phony eggs called 'nest eggs' that trained chickens where to lay eggs.

"He put them in his welded cap—I bet we carried those for two hours!"

When they stopped by another ranch to ask for eggs, the lady just laughed at the eggs and said she could do better and brought the soldiers two chickens.

EGGLESS, MILKLESS, ALMOST FAT-FREE WWII CAKE

Bring to a boil in a heavy saucepan: 1 c brown sugar, 1 c water, 1 c raisins, 2 T oil or margarine, 1 t cinnamon, ½ t cloves Cook gently 5 mins, remove from heat and cool until warm.

Preheat oven to 350 degrees, grease and flour 8x4" baking pan.

Sift together: ½ t salt, ½ t baking powder, ½ t soda

Add to cooled sugar mixture, beat until smooth.

Stir in ½ c chopped walnuts

Spread in baking pan and bake for 25-30 mins, or until a broomstraw inserted in center of cake comes out clean.

Let cool for 10 mins, turn onto a rack to cool completely.

For a good glaze, save back a little spiced water, mix w/ confectioner's sugar, a drop of vanilla, and a pinch of salt. Glaze cake while still warm.

"Nothing is impossible, the word itself says 'I'm possible'!"

Audrey Hepburn

Chapter 7

Margarine: Midwest Wars

When the United States experienced butter shortages in World War II, margarine began to bypass butter commercially. This occurred because of some improvements in its manufacturing process.

Factories began using hydrogenated vegetable oils rather than animal fats in production. They sidestepped the yellow ban by including yellow food coloring when they sold white margarine. According to one nonagenarian, the coloring looked something like jellybeans.

Consumers simply squished the margarine and the coloring together to produce a butter-colored non-butter spread. However, in Wisconsin, where dairy herds flourished, using yellow margarine was declared a crime punishable by fines or imprisonment.

People in the Midwest heard that Eleanor Roosevelt promoted this new margarine product, claiming that she ate margarine on her toast. Many present-day adults recall sitting at the kitchen table to complete one of their chores for the day—mashing the colored tablets into their family's allotment of margarine.

One woman (who prefers to remain anonymous) was ten years old in 1944, and recalls this job in her family's kitchen. Mushing the color into the margarine was just one more task to be accomplished. When the margarine looked comparable in color to real butter from cow's milk, she moved on to another chore.

"This is not the end. It is not even the beginning of the end. But it is, perhaps, the end of the beginning."
Winston Churchill—November 10, 1942

Chapter 8

Rationing: Cinch Up That Belt

O n a WWII poster, an aproned homemaker raises her right hand and pledges: "I pay no more than top legal prices. I accept no rationed goods without giving up ration stamps." The war had entered the kitchens of America.

Of course, sugar was the first food supply to be rationed. The main flow of the imported sweetener stopped in 1942 when the Japanese conquered the Philippines. Shipments from Hawaii, Central and South America were curtailed as cargo vessels were diverted for military purposes because of U-boat submarine attacks.

The nation's sugar supply fell by one-third. The government directed that manufacturers receive eighty percent of pre-war levels, so the military could receive its needed allotments.

On April 27, 1942, civilians registered for ration books at their local elementary schools, only one book per family member. The ration book was to be surrendered upon death. Every

person in the United States received a Ration Book in which stamps were good for one pound of sugar every two weeks over fifty-six weeks. Customers tore off their stamps in the presence of the grocer, and hoarding sugar was frowned upon.

Because canning demands sugar, each person could apply for a twenty-five pound allotment of canning sugar each year. A special stamp was attached to the application for the sugar, but just because the stamp was issued didn't mean that sugar became available to civilians.

In 1945 when Europe was liberated, the US sent food to the war torn continent. On May 1, 1945, US housewives squeezed meals and canning from thirty pounds of sugar for the year. To their credit, American women used corn syrup, flavored gelatin and honey as sweeteners. They understood the posters that claimed: "Rationing means a fair share for all of us."

For Gunpowder

SAVE WASTE FATS

Rush Them to Your Meat Dealer

Butter and oil were also rationed for military reasons. The supply of cooking oil was choked off by Japanese dominance of the Pacific Islands, and the Navy needed fats to grease their guns. By 1943, butter, fats and oils joined the ration list. "Oleo" margarine, with the packet of yellow food dye, replaced real butter.

Glycerin is made from fats and is a crucial ingredient in the manufacture of explosives such as nitroglycerin. Glycerin also was used as a lubricant for planes and tanks, in hydraulics, in the production of food wrappers, in dyes for uniforms and in pharmaceuticals. Because so much glycerin was needed, housewives saved cooking fats, and turned them in at the meat markets.

"One tablespoon of kitchen grease fires five bullets." In 1943, families received two ration points and four cents for each pound of grease reclaimed from cooking. The grease had to be strained through a fine-mesh sieve, be free from water and juices, and not rancid. For the frugal homemaker, this patriotic act satisfied the soul and added ration stamps for other needed food supplies.

Processed foods met the rationed list soon after the war started. Japan controlled seventy percent of the world's tin supply. Tin for civilian use had to be diverted to the military:

ration tins, ammunition boxes, plasma containers, morphine syrettes. On September 17, 1944, processed foods were removed from rationing, but it took several harvests to secure a steady market of tinned foods in the stores.

For a nation that had become caffeine lovers, it was with great joy that coffee was the first of all the rationed items to come off the list on July 28, 1943. At that point, each person was only allowed one pound of coffee every six weeks. Although the home front was willing to sacrifice for the war effort, coffee withdrawal created anxiety for many during the eight months of coffee rationing.

People tried using a level—not heaping—tablespoon per cup to stretch the grounds. Many added chicory to the drink, and to increase the yield, some believed a percolator helped. No one filled the cup to the brim anymore. Most Americans drank less than half of what they previously consumed.

No wonder coffee consumption began with gusto immediately after President Roosevelt announced that coffee rationing was ending. A nation mellowed out. The coffee pot was finally on.

Although the palates of

Americans changed during the war, their attitude toward rationing was summed up in seven words. "Do with less—so they'll have enough."

WHACKY CAKE
From the Family Kitchen of Donna Pronobis, Chicago

Note on recipe: "(This recipe is) From the time of WWII when eggs could be scarce unless you kept chickens, there weren't fifteen different types of flour in the grocery store, and tap water was safe to drink."

Ingredients
- 3 cups sifted flour
- 6 Tablespoons cocoa
- 2 teaspoons baking soda
- 2 cups sugar
- 2 teaspoons salt

Sift above ingredients into 9x13 inch baking pan. Add:
- 12 Tablespoons shortening, melted
- 2 Tablespoons vinegar
- 2 cups cold water
- 2 teaspoons vanilla

Stir all ingredients well in the 9x13 pan. Do NOT beat. Bake for 40 minutes at 350 degrees.

"Do with less…so they'll have enough!"
WWII poster

Chapter 9

Victory Gardens:
They Grow On You

The concept is simple. Fight the enemy with vegetables. Kentucky Wonder pole beans, Glory of Enkhuizen cabbage, Golden Bantam corn, Curled Vates kale, chard, kohlrabi, squash, carrots, potatoes, tomatoes, asparagus, and beets. By 1944, an estimated 20 million victory gardens produced roughly 8 million tons of food, equivalent of more than forty percent of all fresh fruits and vegetables consumed in the United States.

"Our food is fighting," read a U.S. poster. With the goal of lowering the price the vegetables needed to feed the troops, one garden for every seven residents popped up on the American home front. Urbanites pressed every square foot of soil into service. No piece of ground was safe from the relentless hoeing and raking.

School grounds, church

YOUR VICTORY GARDEN
counts more than ever!

yards, front lawns, and back alleys grew green from the relentless seeding. Any pot that could hold dirt balanced on fire escapes and balconies with the promise of delectable veggies. Empty lots transformed into community gardens.

Rooftops on sturdy buildings proved perfect places to harvest sun-loving crops. The hope that the vegetables would provide nutrition during the winter months spurred civic organizations to participate in the Victory Gardens project.

Even the White House eventually planted a garden on the elegant lawns. Eleanor Roosevelt wanted to join the country by turning grass into productive food acreage. President Roosevelt told the soil scientists paid to test the White House soil. "Tell her the yard is full of rocks or something. The people own this place and don't want it busted up just so she can plant beans." FDR liked his green expanses of grass.

In March, 1943, the White House grounds finally joined the nation in planting a wartime garden. Diana Hopkins, daughter of Secretary of Commerce Harry L. Hopkins, would use the flowerbeds to grow a harvest of vegetables. "It will be a small thing," Mrs. Roosevelt said. "Children can grow things they are apt to want to grow in a very small space." Eventually, the Roosevelts maintained an expertly managed vegetable garden that produced copious amounts of organic vegetables for the First Family's table.

Farm families had been planting gardens and preserving produce for generations. But in the name of patriotism, the city folks joined them in the seasonal planting and harvesting through Victory Gardens. In the heyday of women's magazines, many articles gave instructions to the general public on how to garden as well as how to use pressure cookers safely.

In 1943, the effort to preserve the harvest escalated.

Families bought 315,000 pressure cookers to use with the Ball Blue Book of Canning.

Kelly Holthus, a ten year-old in 1943, recalls the Victory Gardens planted by his parents on a farm in Nebraska. "It was a great moral thing."

He knew that the garden helped his family make their rations go further and also helped the troops to eat well. "In the cities, and even in the country everybody wanted to have their own garden, to raise their own produce and maybe have enough (to give to) somebody who didn't have access to a garden."[1]

Like other boys growing up during the war, Kelly Holthus never forgot the patriotic spirit and hard work of his parents' generation to take part in the home-front effort in practical ways. Fighting an enemy by raising harvests of produce to feed a nation: the ultimate food fight.

VEGETABLE LOAF
From *Economy Recipes for Canada's "Housesoldiers*
Toronto: Canada Starch, 1943

Ingredients
 2 cups cooked carrots, diced
 2 ½ cups cooked lima or navy beans, mashed
 2 large eggs
 1 tsp salt
 ¼ tsp pepper
 Dash Cayenne pepper
 ¼ tsp Worcestershire sauce
 ½ cup milk
 3 cups bread crumbs, not too stale
 ½ onion, chopped fine
 4 Tbsp melted fat
 2 Tbsp chopped parsley

Instructions
 Combine cooked, diced carrots and cooked mashed beans.
 Beat eggs slightly, add seasonings and milk.
 Combine breadcrumbs, chopped onion, melted fat and parsley: add to vegetables mixing thoroughly.
 Turn into well-greased loaf pan and bake at 375 degrees for 35 to 40 minutes. Serves 4-6 people.

Getty Stewart, speaker and writer, has tested this recipe from WWII. She is a Professional Home Economist and gardener.

"If we grow for our homes, farmers can grow for our armed forces."

Chapter 10

Canning:

Preserving the Harvest

Summer and fall equals canning season. For many home-makers, the rhythm of the seasons had never stopped. These frugal women had canned food all through the Great Depression and into WWII. The only difference lay in the fact that no one canned lamb's ears or other weeds as they did in the Dust Bowl a decade before.

Victory Gardens produced voluminous vegetables to "put up" in jars in order to stock the shelves for winter consumption. An average of 165 jars per household were canned each year.

For the rest of the population who had not been raised in a rural area, the USDA created 6,000 canning centers throughout the United States. Each facility offered instructional and educational supervision from women knowledgeable in canning. The use of water bath and pressure cookers under guidance insured a safe product.

Individuals brought their harvest from the Victory Garden and paid a small fee to use the equipment. This offered an important service to families who wanted to do their part in the war effort. In 1944, the USDA estimated that nearly four billion jars of food were produced from local harvests and canned by 75% of the country's housewives.

Many vegetables need pressure cooker canners to be safely preserved. *Presto Pressure Cookers*, made in Eau Claire, Wisconsin, converted much of its production facility into the war effort. But throughout the conflict, the company still manufactured pressure canners for the victory garden and community canning programs.

These canners, made of steel rather than aluminum, allowed housewives to preserve vegetables safely in their own kitchens. All winter long, mothers fed their children food grown in backyard gardens.

The Blue Book of Canning by the Ball jar company became the classic reference book for these patriotic canners. The thin book was written in simple terms for the layperson to understand. Easy to reference recipes had been tested for success. Now, any woman in the United States could easily stock up on bread and butter pickles, strawberry jam, tomato sauce, applesauce, ketchup, peach halves, asparagus stalks, pickled beets, and more.

In the midst of rationing, filling the larder with colorful jars of nutritious vittles empowered homemakers on the home front. Even as the war years morphed into peacetime, the women of America continued to grow gardens and can their bounty.

The lure of locally grown vegetables flavored according to a family's preference kept home canners busy until mid-century. For GIs back from deployment, nothing tasted as delicious as a bowl of sun-ripened peaches when winter snow blew outside.

Sunshine in a jar.

> *"But there is one front and one battle where everyone in the United States–every man, woman and child–is in action. That front is right here at home, in our daily lives."*
>
> President Franklin D. Roosevelt, 1942

Chapter 11

Women's Land Army:
Women's Work

N ails that had been carefully filed and polished a week before now plunged into composted soil with onion sets planted for a harvest. A bandana held hair that had once been maintained in a salon. Overalls replaced the cotton dresses and stylish suits of the office.

America's women joined first lady Eleanor Roosevelt in an effort to ensure that the nation's wartime food production goals were met. The Women's Land Army marched into the fields, groves, hatcheries and orchards to grow the produce needed for their sons, husbands, brothers and fathers serving across the ocean.

When volunteers showed up for seasonal work on farms to weed, thin, prune or harvest, the women included accountants, actresses, artists, bank clerks, beauticians, nurses, research chemists, translators, and recruits from all vocations of life. Over 1.5 million nonfarm women participated in the Women's Land Army during the war.[1]

The farmers, whose sons had been deployed to fight overseas, could not have harvested the crops without the help of these women. A Midwestern farmer stated: "I will say that they were eminently successful and helped me get the job done…They drove tractors for me on side rake, pick-up baler, rotary hoe and trucks to pick up hay in the field…The boys in the armed forces should know the remarkable work done by these women and farmer's wives."[2]

As more and more farmers departed from rural America to join the military or work in the war industry, the women who lived on the nation's six million farms shouldered the responsibilities of planting, cultivating and harvesting the nation's crops. Foreign workers from Mexico, the Bahamas and Canada were imported to help and some prisoners of war were allowed to harvest in the Heartland.

Military personnel received furloughs for short amounts of time to help in North Dakota, Maine and New York. Conscientious objectors as well as Japanese persons in relocation centers worked in the agricultural industry, as well as Japanese persons in relocation centers. All of these joined with the Women's Land Army to produce the food needed for a nation, a military, and a world at war.

As one WLA recruitment poster proclaimed: "War takes food—Food for our fighting men. Food for our fighting allies. Food for workers at home…We need more hands. Enroll now in the Women's Land Army."

Office workers were encouraged to plot "their vacation plans against a calendar of crop seasons to help get in the food our army must have, our allies must have, our workers must have, the people at home must have." Many of these recruits participated in one-day programs in which they traveled back and forth in buses or carpools. Others lived in camps or on farms. All worked hard at the challenges of agriculture.

Under the hot summer sun, these volunteers raised vegetables in the rocky New England soil. They topped onions in Michigan's fields. Manicured hands detasseled the corn crop of the Midwest. In North Dakota, workers shocked wheat. In the South, they picked cotton. Up in Maine, they dug potatoes.

Fruits ripened and were harvested in every state. All across the nation, female hands milked cows and collected eggs. These sturdy women, the unsung heroines of the food front, embraced every aspect of farm life.

As one recruit recalled, "No matter how heavy the hay we pitched, how our backs ached from weeding, or how stubborn the team we were driving, we always had the secret joy that we were helping the war effort."[3]

The contribution of women to agriculture is one of the least known aspects of World War II in the United States. If these Women of the Land Army had not volunteered to plow, cultivate and harvest the crops, food would have been scarcer for both the home front and the fighting men.

The physical strength of the military would have been compromised. The allies, who already suffered from food shortages, would have faced starvation. Rationing and food shortages would have created health problems. But because of the WLA, these consequences were avoided.

In a grassroots movement, the women of America came "to rescue the crops." Housewives, college students, teenagers, secretaries, and farm mothers expended their energy and ingenuity. As a grateful President Roosevelt said: "Food is the life line of the forces that fight for freedom."

Mary Ross recalls the remarks of her father, a North Carolina farmer who depended upon Land Army recruits. "Men may have fought to defend the land, but women toiled it. Women saved our heritage."[4]

An honorary salute to the Women's Land Army!

HOMITY PIE
A Land Girls Specialty
This dish was enjoyed during WWII because it is a frugal vegetarian main dish. This recipe is a traditional British pie filling that dates to pre-war baking, but resembles the one used by the Lands Girls during wartime rationing.

Ingredients:
   1 Tablespoon of vegetable oil
   2 ½ cups of white potatoes, peeled and cubed
   2 large diced onions
   3 minced cloves of garlic
   3 sliced large leeks
   ¼ cup chopped red pepper
   1 ½ cup frozen peas
   ½ cup diced carrots
   2 cups sliced mushrooms
   ½ cup vegetable stock
   1 ½ cup sharp cheddar cheese
   Salt, pepper, parsley and thyme to taste

Method of Cooking
   Grease deep pie dish with oil. Set aside.
   Boil the potatoes, drain and mash. Set aside.
   Cook onions, leeks, mushrooms and peas until soft in fry pan.
   To the fry pan, add the mashed potatoes, diced veggies, garlic, herbs, eggs, stock, and half the cheese. Stir until combined throughout.
   Transfer this mixture into the greased pie dish. Cover with the remaining cheese.

Bake for 20 minutes in 400 degrees F. Watch for the cheese to brown, but be careful not to let it burn.

Precooked bacon bits or scraps of ham can be added to the recipe to provide flavor and extra protein, but is not part of the traditional Land Girls recipe.

Makes 2 small pies, or one large pie. Serves 6.

"We're working for Victory, too; growing food for ourselves and our countrymen. While other women work at machines and in factories, we're soldiers in overalls…We're running the place while Dad's away."
Toni Taylor,
"Women on the Home Front"
McCalls, May, 1942

Chapter 12

Refrigerators:
Tips From the Experts

Many American factories transformed their production lines in order to aid to war effort. Workers who once manufactured automobiles, woodstoves or lamps now produced weapons of warfare to speed the Allied victory.

But companies still cared about their customers and looked forward to peacetime, evidenced in the foreword to a small leaflet published by the Frigidaire Company in 1943.

Benito Mussolini banned the sale of ice cream in Italy because it was 'too American.'

Adapted from *Ice Cream*, by Robert T. Marshall, H. 2003, Second Edition, 2013. Additional Authors: H. Douglas Goff, and Richard W. Hartel

Chapter 13

Farm Life During the War

Leone Dunkelberg grew up on a Southern Iowa farm in Iowa County. Born in 1927, she shares vivid memories of World War II. Producing enough food for their family of five children and making a living required all of her parents' energies.

She recalls making sausage using the intestines of pigs for casings, cooking down the skins for cracklings, and rendering lard after her father butchered a cow or hog. He made dried beef, ham and bacon in the smokehouse and salted down pork. He also covered fresh pork with lard to seal it. The family saved every bit of grease produced through frying, and her parents made soap with grease and lye in a big black kettle over a fire in the yard.

Leone's mother canned jars of fresh-butchered beef. She also used a sauerkraut cutter over a crock to preserve cabbage for winter use. When to the correct sourness, she would can it in glass jars, using a rubber ring and zinc lid.

Neighboring farm families worked together to

67

thresh the harvest, and in the fall, celebrated their community with a big oyster stew supper—this was the menu on Christmas Eve, also. Leone attributes this to the influence of so many German immigrants, but wonders why they would import oysters when other meats were so plentiful.

The family preserved wild chokecherries for jelly and syrup, and ate elderberries, black walnuts and hickory nuts. At the beginning of the war, rural electrification came into vogue, and Leone's mother faced a difficult choice.

"Mother had used a wood stove her whole life, and just couldn't believe she could cook on an electric stove. So my parents bought a dual model—half wood stove, half electric.

In June of 1943, FDR signed the Nurse Training Act due to a shortage in civilian nurses. By July, the Cadet Nurse Corps evolved—these cadets wore army style winter and summer uniforms and trained at Iowa Lutheran Hospital in Des Moines. As she says, "The government paid for tuition, books, food, and provided a place to stay."

Leone entered the program, but by the time she finished her training, the war had ended. She notes that the government kept its promise to complete the cadets' training, but stopped issuing uniforms to these last graduates.

Still, she honed an impressive array of life skills, some from the Cadet Nurse Corps, others from her farm background. Living close to the land during the early years of the war, many children like Leone carried on their parents' industrious lifestyles through adulthood.

"*It was a feeling of pride that I started my day as a farmer helper. And so it went, load after load, day after day, until I have now hauled over 10,000 bushels of corn. Tired? Of course, I get tired, but so does that boy in the foxhole. That boy, whose place I'm trying so hard to fill.*"

Mrs. Leslie Tresham of Hornick, Iowa

The Military

Introduction

The U.S. military classifies everything, including food. In World War II, soldiers ate rations, beginning with the meals served in garrison duty. These were labeled Class A, with fresh vegetables, meat, poultry and fruit. Class B consisted of canned meat, vegetables, and fruit served in the field.

Class C rations were originally conceived as "A balanced meal in a can," and employed six 12-ounce cans. Three contained meat and bread units. The others provided sugar, soluble instant coffee and hard candy. One day's rations offered 3,000 calories.

Although efforts were made to introduce greater variety, three major C ration components remained throughout the war—meat and beans, meat and vegetable hash, and vegetable

Introduction

stew. But soldiers had difficulty eating these rations cold and carrying the six bulky cans.

The Army also issued D rations for extreme emergencies, (for example, Normandy during the first few days after soldiers arrived.) D rations provided three four-ounce chocolate bars fortified with sucrose, skim milk, cacao fat and oatmeal flour and contained 1,800 calories each.

K rations were created by Dr. Ancel Keys, a nutritionist at the University of Minnesota who received a request from the War Department in 1940. War had begun in Europe, so the Department asked Dr. Key to create a nutritious paratrooper ration. Soldiers at Fort Snelling first tested K rations, followed by other tests at Fort Benning, GA before this ration became the standard field issue for the war's duration.

Packaged in three rectangular boxes that could fit into a paratrooper's pocket, each box held a separate meal including crackers, dextrose tablets, a can of meat and egg or processed meat, and a stick of chewing gum. Another box contained a fruit bar, soluble concentrated bouillon, a 2-ounce D-ration bar, lemonade powder, sugar tablets and a small toilet paper roll.

The lemonade and concentrated coffee were the first of their kinds. The breakfast box offered a bar of fruit, figs and raisins for regularity and the noon lunch can supplied cheese to prevent loose bowels. The K ration could be eaten repeatedly without getting tiresome.

The quartermasters also designed the 5 in 1 ration to feed five men for one day. These warm meals could easily be prepared by novices. One soldier, Philip A. Langehough, wrote, "A breakfast would consist of dehydrated tomato juice, whole-wheat cereal, soluble coffee, sugar and canned milk, and the best canned bacon I ever ate.

"With the cereal, all you had to do was open the box and add water to the dry milk found on the cereal. We would have a K-ration for lunch, and dinner would include meat and vegetable stew, vanilla pudding powder or canned glorified rice whipped cream, and pineapple, a supply of biscuits, and a fruit spread. The nutrition value of all this food was a whopping 3,668 calories.

"A small can opener was issued with the 5 in 1 rations. It measured 1½ inches by 1/16, a blade opened each can with minimum effort. I still have one placed under glass with the rest of my Army decorations."

PFC Langehough also describes Army cooks' special efforts in the field to provide a dessert for an otherwise drab diet. They made extra pancake batter in the mornings, added sugar, vanilla, and other ingredients to make a cake. After baking, they added peanut butter and orange marmalade for frosting.

In a 1945 letter, Langehough described his third and last Thanksgiving Day abroad as his unit awaited transport back to the States. "…celebrated in typical army fashion. Breakfast at 7:30, church at 11:00, and the big meal at 4:30. The meal consisted of one pound of turkey per man, dressing, mashed potato, giblet gravy, asparagus, coffee, rolls, ice cream, apple pie, and fruitcake."

He added that the meal was well cooked, that he was stuffed until 10 p.m., but that some of the men were still hungry and took half of a turkey to eat in their rooms. We can only imagine how these soldiers had hungered for turkey and dressing during their long months of battle.

(*When Hearts Were Brave Again and Arms Were Strong*, pp. 197-200, Philip A. Langehough, PFC, Information International, 2005.)

Chapter 14

Soldiers in the Field

Accounts of soldiers in the field invariably include comments about food. The standard military rations (C-Rations or C-Rats) provided 4,000 calories per day in three meals for an active soldier. K-Rations, lighter for shorter missions, provided 2,830 calories in three meals.

Needless to say, soldiers became experts at scrounging for additional nutrition. From making soup with nettles to hunting wild game and roasting it over a campfire, innovations became endless.

Besides meal times, the best hour of the day was mail call. Imagine a soldier receiving a care package from home filled with homemade cookies or fudge—what a heartwarming moment!

One eighteen year-old infantry private's recollections provide a glimpse of how much food meant to the troops. Especially after the enemy captured his unit in Northern France, hunger became even more rampant.

"Summer 1944—training at Ft. Kilmar, New York: This was an exciting time to be in a place like New York City. Huge signs gave a running account of the war, and everywhere you turned there were GIs. It seemed like we had invaded the big apple. I also remember that the food was fabulous. And over the next several months, I thought of that fact often.

"September 1944—on the transport ship, *La France* (an eleven day trip from New York City to Liverpool, with approximately 20,000 soldiers, WACS and staff on board):

"I spent most of my time below decks, cutting bread. This was my job on the ship, cutting bread. This may seem trivial until you realize that we went through about 900 loaves of fresh-baked bread a day on that ship. But due to the damp conditions, some of the bread began to rot.

"As the trip drew to a close, I asked about this moldy bread. I was told to cut off the worst and feed it to them anyway, but I ended up throwing it out. I guess it wouldn't hurt anybody, I just figured if a guy was about to go into war, he didn't need to be eating moldy bread."

After liberating many French villages in the fight across Normandy toward Germany, this soldier was captured. His experience shows the Nazi's fundamental disregard for the Geneva Convention concerning Prisoners of War, including those concerning nutrition.

Article II

The food ration for prisoners of war shall be equal quantity and quality to that of troops at base camps. Furthermore, prisoners shall receive facilities preparing, themselves, additional food which they might have. A sufficiency of potable water shall be furnished them...

Article XII

Canteens shall be installed in all camps where prisoners may obtain, at the local market price, food products and ordinary objects.

Notes from a small German village

"Following the most recent wave of allied bombings, we stayed in this town for a few days to help clean up. One day a German guard came into the house and asked for help taking some people out of buildings that had been destroyed. As we walked down the street, nearly every building had been affected by the bombings.

"Around dinnertime, we were taken to an area where they had a big kettle, maybe twenty or thirty gallons of soup. This guard told us that we could eat as long as he did, but when he stopped, we had to stop. I ate six bowls to his one, but when he quit, so did we. I think I could have eaten another six bowls.

En route across Germany to final camp

"Because of the importance of food, one thing stands out in my memory during these seemingly ceaseless days on the dirt roads of Germany. When you have not had a decent meal for days and sometimes weeks, the thought of food consumes your mind. Sometimes it is all you ever think of.

This mental state plus the obvious loss of physical strength made for a relatively miserable existence. On one occasion I remember looking over and seeing an apple tree and there were APPLES! The telltale ball-shaped mounds covered with a light sifting of snow called to us...We must have been quite a spectacle, a group of grown men, haggard and hardened by war scrambling and digging like children to get our share of this unexpected feast.

Remember, it was late December at this point, and we grabbed for these apples excited beyond belief that they still appeared edible. Of course, by this time it did not take much to be edible.

I'm not sure how, but I did manage to get a couple for myself. Just as we were ready to sink our teeth into the somewhat hard treat, the German guards told us not to eat the apples because they might make us sick.

Now, think how ridiculous that sounded to us. We figured that we were going to die anyway, either from starvation or dehydration or marching or by the Germans, so getting a stomachache was the least of our concerns.

I hate to say it, but those guards were right. A lot of us got a bad case of dysentery from those apples. This of course only added to our weakened condition."

At Stalag X11 A, Limberg, Germany, northeast of Koblenz
"My condition was deteriorating rapidly by this time due to the combination of mental stress and physical exertion. We were welcomed to our new home by the sight of barbed wire, guard towers, and what passed for our barracks. In actuality, these barracks were hardly livable.

"During my stay in Limberg, we were given very little to eat or drink, usually something passed off as soup, but was mostly dirty colored water which did very little to appease your appetite or thirst. I received virtually no water or food.

"...there were thousands of us, with prisoners from all over the globe, Indians, Russians, and some from Italy. Each nationality had a compound of its own, so we really had little contact with anyone other than Americans and our German guards.

"The facilities ... were on par with livestock buildings back in Iowa. No beds or bathrooms, only a bit of old lice-infested straw if you were lucky, and a five-gallon bucket in the middle for a bathroom. It is impossible for most people to imagine the lack of food and water...

"When you consider that the bucket would not fill up during the day, even with so many men, it's clear we were not being treated well. Most of us hardly ever went to the bathroom.

"Of course, the war was nearing the end, and the Germans had little in the way of food themselves, but I still think they could have done more. When we got out, the nurses at the hospital referred to us as walking skeletons."

On a work detail

"The day of this particular incident, several hundred of us were trudging along a road like we had done so many times before. This road must have been cut along a rock bank, as one side was a collection of rock outcroppings reaching out toward our column. Somewhere toward the end of our procession, I was double shocked when I spied what appeared to be a loaf of bread sitting on one of the numerous ledges along the road.

"Here within an arm's reach, a loaf of bread covered with a light dusting of snow had gone unnoticed by several hundred starving prisoners until I came along. You can bet that I didn't ask questions or pass up this golden opportunity.

"I looked around and figured I just as well eat it as anyone. At this point, this was truly a miracle for me, as I had nearly given up hope. My mother was a very religious person, and she was always praying for me. I don't know if that has anything to do with that loaf of bread, but something had done it.

Another story from Limberg

Perhaps the most cruel aspect of my stay at Limberg was not the lack of food, but witnessing others getting food through various Red Cross parcels. One of the rules governing war allows POWs to receive aid from various organizations, like the Red Cross.

"During my period of service, I was to receive occasional parcels, kind of like a care package usually including some food and toiletries, but never got a single parcel the whole time I was in captivity. This would not be that big of a deal, but I watched as some of the prisoners from India and Russia got the parcels that were intended for us Americans.

"Some of the guys would give up their wedding rings or other items of value in exchange for a little food from these parcels. I never did. I couldn't see paying for something that was by all rights mine in the first place."

After rescue by American troops

"Many of the GIs tried to aid us in our recovery by giving us some food and water. We were told, as strange as this sounds, not to eat too much. After 100 days of little food, dreaming of the day when I could eat, consumed by the thought of food, the good guys are now telling me not to eat too much?

"Later I was told that because of my condition that if I had eaten too much it would have made me sick and possibly even been fatal. Thankfully I did as I was told. I do remember the first piece of white bread that I ate…it was heaven. I didn't know anything could taste so good.

"From Bergsolms, Germany where I was liberated, we were put on an ambulance and taken to an American field hospital. While there, I was put into a bed with three other guys, just a standard bed and four grown men. This shows how much body weight we had lost during our ordeal.

"I had gone from one hundred and fifty or sixty pounds to approximately ninety-five pounds upon liberation. My teeth had turned rubbery, so I received a lot of dental work when we arrived in England."

From *MY 100 DAYS Of HELL*, The Story of John A. Bauer. G&R Publishing Company, Waverly, IA 50677 (No copyright date available)

The diary of an eighteen-year old farm boy-turned Special Forces/Alamo Scouts provides a steady stream of comments like, "Reconnoitered on beach. Climbed into jungle, killed seven Japs. Slept in pouches in jungle. Ants ate us alive."

This GI trained in New Guinea for General Kruger's special unit for behind-the-lines maneuvers. These paratroopers dropped in behind enemy lines and disappeared into the jungle or whatever else covered the terrain. They participated in raids on the enemy, gathered information vital to the command, and in the case of this particular soldier, played a vital rose in the successful raid on the Japanese POW camp holding the survivors of the Bataan Death March.

This soldier's scribbled remarks give the sense of his detachment's daily life. One can almost smell these grimy guerilla fighters packed into an LCI heading for an island beach, scrabbling through jungle paths infested with insects and disease, being summoned at a moment's notice to pack up and head somewhere else for a new mission, spending a day fixing a radio or cleaning a tent, playing cards, checkers, or volleyball to pass the time before a night march twelve-hours long.

These young men carried K-rations, which left something to be desired. Throughout the diary, bright spots often have to do with food.

"Disembarked. Proceeded by truck to 7th Cavalry area. No passes, placed on alert."

"Heat intense. Fired on range. Qualified as sharpshooter. Compass course and new bayonet training. Plenty of milk to drink."

"Same training schedule and working on tents. Tommy got tooth pulled."

"Laid up—ears swollen." Two days later ... "In hospital, ears treated. Red Cross package—cigarettes, gum, candy."

"Saw show. 'Princess and the Pirates' with Bob Hope. Four coca colas from PX. Beer ration supposed to show up soon."

"My whole outfit on K.P. biggest mess hall I've ever seen. Had hygiene lecture."

"Moved out. One Jap plane overhead. Laid in Gulf. Seen bombardment troops capture airstrip in twenty minutes. Seen cruiser Portland and battleships California and West Virginia."

"Set up camp. Went hunting. Cooked pigeons over fire. Pretty tasty."

"Waiting Lieutenant Peel to return from briefing. Read *Riders Purple Sage* and *Wildfire*. Got twelve Hershey candy bars. Helps relieve hunger—chow is good but two meals a day isn't enough."

Days later ... "Rationing my candy bars—two per day. Slept in pouch in jungle. No sleep. Scared. Thought heard Japs. Eating K Rations."

"Rested today. Food dropped by parachute. No food since breakfast yesterday. Candy gone. Welcome sight, those C-47's."

"Broke camp 5:30 a.m. Took off at dawn in C-47. Destination unknown. Seen Jap planes. Artillery fire destroyed one. Set up camp and wrote letters rest of day. Chow terrible."

"Furlough cancelled. Placed on alert. Returned to first scout position. Chow now worth a damn."

"Flew from Luzon to unnamed port. Traveled by native canoe to new post at night. Climb. Guerillas encountered Japs—killed four."

"Working detail. No mail call."

"Helped Lt. instruct men on rocket launcher. Ordered to attack Hill # __—killed two Japs. Knocked out machine gun."

"Attempted to cross rivers. Jap sniper. Returned. Two days. New orders. Moving out."

"Won $5 playing five card stud. Sighted land. Don't know what or where."

"Docked in night. Australia. Seen first wallabe. Back mail arrived—one letter made me mad. Aussie ice cream excellent."

Another Iowan, Dr. Ralph Emerson Hibbs from Oskaloosa, surgeon of the Second Battalion of the 31st Infantry Regiment stationed in the Philippines, described additions to his diet in a letter to his parents. "…The food is fair—carabao, monkey, and occasionally mule…"

The Des Moines Register published his letter, and parts of it appear in *Ghost Soldiers* by Hampton Sides. (Doubleday, 2001.) p.38

Ghost Soldiers also lists the "progressively stranger" meals for the men on Bataan as the Japanese gained control. "Meals consisted of cats, slugs, rats, various dried insects, and the meat and eggs of python." P.39

When the Rangers crawled their way to the Cabanatuan prison camp on Bataan in the Philippines, the command sent along K rations.

They also gave foil-wrapped bars of Hershey's milk chocolate to present to the prisoners as a gift on their

way out of the prison camp if the raid succeeded. P.69
Ghost Soldiers

It takes little thought to realize how important cooks were to our troops. Private James Crosby, who served as a Navy cook in the Pacific Theater and left the war as a Ship's Cook Third Class, describes a precedent-changing decision. (As told to his daughter, Ruth Crosby Newton of Pine, AZ.)

"I was a cook for the Navy stationed in the Marshall Islands. I was brought up to one of my superior officers and asked why the men were not getting any hot chocolate, or milk during meals. I told him that there were not enough ingredients to make a decent hot chocolate or milk. I told the officer, 'It will just taste like water ,so they won't get any till I can make a decent drink for them.'

There were also other items we were short on for decent meals, and I just held back things till more came in so could feed the men correctly. The officer said, "If the men don't get hot chocolate, milk, etc then the officers won't either. So use what is needed from the officers' rations. We are not any better than our men. So I did just that, all got the same meals and drinks as long as I was the cook."

Ernie Pyle, a journalist, wrote from Tunisia, North Africa in 1943. (Ernest Taylor Pyle wrote a syndicated column as a roving reporter for Scripps-Howard Newspapers. He sent his articles from war zones and was killed by a Japanese sniper on June 18,1945 on the Pacific Island of Le Shima in the Ryukyus.)

The following quote is included in the Reader's Digest Illustrated Story of World War II. The Reader's Digest Association, Inc. Pleasantville, New York, 1969.

"The men have been very well cared for in this war. I

suppose no soldiers in any other war in history had such excellent attention as our men overseas. The food is good. Of course we're always yapping about how wonderful a steak would taste on Broadway, but when a soldier is pinned right down he'll admit ungrudgingly that it's Broadway he's thinking about more than the steak, and that he really can't kick on the food. Furthermore, cooking is good in this war. Last time good food was spoiled by lousy cooking, but that is the exception this time. Of course, there are times in battle when the men live for days on nothing but those deadly, cold C rations out of tin cans, and even go without food for a day or two, but these are the crises, the exceptions. On the whole, we figure by the letters from home that we're probably eating better than you are."

Chapter 15

M&M's and Chocolate

Military food provided nutrition, but lacked taste appeal. A snack for the MRE (Meals Ready to Eat) needed to be delicious, energy producing and not affected by temperature. The US military searched for just the right treat to put into the packs.

Forrest Mars, a candy maker in Great Britain, developed an ideal product.

In 1932, Forrest Mars moved to England where he manufactured the iconic Mars bar, Milky Way. During the Spanish Civil War, he noticed the soldier' field kits contained a chocolate product that gave the troops quick energy. Small chocolate beads were encased in a hard sugar shell which prevented the candy from melting.

He developed a version of this treat just as the United States prepared to go to war. Knowing that cocoa and sugar would be rationed, he invited R. Bruce Murrie, a son of the Hershey's Chocolates president, to join him in producing this new candy. They decided to call it M&M for Mars and Murrie. Hershey guaranteed a steady supply of chocolate and a lot of technical help to develop the shelled chocolate.

In 1942, Mars obtained the patent to make the M&Ms and production began in Newark, New Jersey. The small round candies were coated with brown, red, orange, yellow, green and violet colored sugar. They were packed in cardboard tubes. In an interview, Mars claimed that the "thing is they melt in your mouth but they don't melt in your hand." This became the logo of the new candy.

When the US government entered the war, the candy was exclusively sold to the military. The GIs easily hooked onto this quick snack that resisted the excessive heat from battle-fields. M&Ms were produced at a rate of 200,000 pounds a week, and by the end of the war, 600,000 pounds a week. The MRE included a tube for every meal.

When the GIs returned to the States after the war, stores stocked their shelves with brown paper containers of the beloved M&Ms. What a sweet reminder of comrades and close fellowship among a band of brothers!

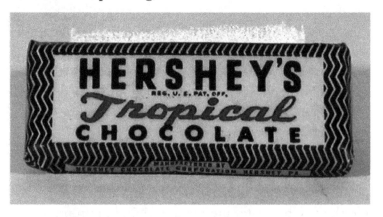

Chocolate Bars

Commercially processed chocolate bars sold rapidly in the PX, the most popular item after cigarettes. The chocolate bar is associated with troops in the European theater, where the precious candy translated into an all-purpose medium of exchange for goods and services. Even the D Ration bars could be used for bargaining. They fit in a soldier's pocket, although they were not always tasty and hard to chew. But D Ration bars were calorie-laden and just what a hungry population craved.

Both types of chocolate turned many hungry Europeans into friends of the United States. "People wanted them," said John Otto, 82nd Airborne Division's 505th Parachute Regiment. "You'd give them to kids. In some places they were very hungry. And they sure helped relax people about American soldiers."

For some war weary civilians, even the Field Ration D was appreciated. Audrey Hepburn lived in Holland, on the edge of starvation for several years. Her body carried the pain of the war for the rest of her life. The GIs who shared chocolate with her at the end of the war saved her life. Audrey's son recalls: "The taste of chocolate for her was connected with liberation. It was the real taste of freedom."

Chocolate, it seems, is the answer. Who cares what the question is.

"The soldier above all others prays for peace, for it is the soldier who must suffer and bear the deepest wounds and scars of war."
Douglas Macarthur

Chapter 16

Ration D Bar

T he officer had chocolate on his mind.

Colonel Paul Logan, deputy director of the subsistence division of the US Army's Office of the Quartermaster General watched his troops and saw the need for a candy bar to provide a quick, high-calorie energy boost in the midst of intense conflict. In the spring of 1937, he approached the Hersey Chocolate factory with his proposal to provide a chocolate bar that soldiers would want to eat only in dire situations.

Logan wanted the troops to "Keep calm and eat chocolate" when under fire. He asked that the bar taste only "a little better than a boiled potato." The Hershey Company succeeded, because many a soldier quipped, "I'd rather eat the boiled potato." The D Ration was nicknamed "Hitler's Secret Weapon" for the gastrointestinal havoc it produced.

Four requirements from the military faced Hershey's chief chemist, Sam Hinkle. Create a four–ounce, 600 calorie bar that would withstand high temperatures and not tempt GIs in a non-combat situation. Hinkle unveiled the Field Ration D chocolate bar blended from chocolate, sugar, cocoa butter, oat flour and skim milk.

The resulting dense bars threatened to chip the teeth of those who bit into them. Most shaved off curls with their knives, savoring the sweet, yet bitter cocoa flavor. Crumbling the D bar into a cup of boiling water and drinking the result-ing beverage reminded them of cold winter nights back home.

The Pacific Theater's extreme heat challenged the melt-ing point of the D bar. In 1943, the Hershey Corporation created the Tropical Chocolate Bar, which was packaged in one to two ounce sizes. A bit tastier than the Ration D bars, the Tropical Bar stood up to the heat and energized men serving in the jungle.

Hershey churned out 24 million bars per week, producing 3 billion ration bars by the end of the war. The Hersey Cor-poration was awarded the Army-Navy "E" Production award for their efforts in supplying the troops with the power they needed when under fire.

Military medical personnel worked around the clock trying to save the lives of wounded GIs, with barely time to eat rations, much less a hot meal served on a metal plate. Many times, their growling stomachs told the tale of their hunger. Despite their need to eat, these men and women stayed focused on their medical tasks. Ration D bars pro-vided something to chew on between changing ban-dages or hooking up an IV.

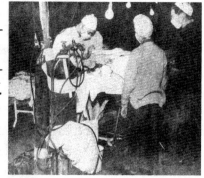

Instant energy. Never underestimate the power of chocolate.

A Chocolate Story

Marc Worst of Lockport, Illinois tells this story about his mother, a surgical nurse with the U.S. Army's Eleventh Evacuation Hospital. I

"In July of 1943, a Sicilian man brought his goats to the hospital's encampment. He came to my mom's tent but she was sleeping. He wiggled her toes to wake her (her feet sometimes stuck out from the small tent).

When she sat up, he asked if she wanted some goat milk and she said she did. So she tried a little and realized it had a different taste. She tried to improve the taste by adding a chocolate bar to the milk in her helmet and heating it like hot chocolate, but that made it worse, so she got rid of it."

Ingredients of the Field Ration D bar
  Chocolate
  Oat flour
  Cacao fat
  Skim milk powder
  Sugar
  Vanillin crystals

"Good soldiers never pass up a chance to eat or sleep. They never know how much they'll be called on to do before the next chance."
Lois McMaster Bujold

Chapter 17

Doughnut Dolly

On the fifth of May 1943, Angela "Angie" Petesch began "the most interesting time of my life." With sixty-eight other Red Cross volunteers, she made her way to England to give aid to the troops in outlying sections of Europe. They traveled in Clubmobiles supplied with the makings of donuts and cups of coffee.

The *Doughnut Dollies,* as they were affectionately called, lived in small uncelebrated villages or out in the field close

to battle. Because of them, the lowly fried doughnut became a symbol of the Red Cross's goal to ease the hardships of the frontline fighting man.

"With its clubs for recreation, its coffee and doughnuts in the forward areas... (with) the devotion and warmhearted sympathy of the Red Cross girl, the Red Cross has often seemed to be the friendly hand of this nation, reaching across the sea to sustain its fighting men."- Allied Commander Dwight D. Eisenhower, 1945

When the World War II Red Cross volunteers brought coffee and doughnuts to men in war torn areas of Europe, they touched the hearts and souls of American servicemen

and women. This seemingly domestic duty was truly an heroic endeavor.

The men admitted that the Doughnut Dollies "being there gave them a nice warm feeling." That emotion inspired the uniformed pastry- makers to work ten to twelve hours a day from London's foggy streets to the Normandy invasion and on to the snowy forest of the Ardennes. These brave women wanted to be with the troops, not back home waiting for them to return.

The caravan of Red Cross Doughnut Dollies followed the GIs through most of the war's defining moments. They served close to the troops after D-Day, and near Verdun. With thirty-one girls in a group, the volunteers manned Clubmobiles, supply trucks, a Cinemobile and water trailers, generators and tents.

Each Red Cross worker could drive a two and a half ton truck, live in tents, and work in snow and rain while wincing only a bit at the big guns exploding in the near countryside. Still looking feminine, they could talk about tanks, airplanes and rifles as well as movies and music.

Most importantly, they served strong hot coffee and doughnuts they made from scratch in the middle of a cornfield. Angela Petesch boasted that her caravan of Doughnut Dollies served 2,500 donuts a day. The Doughnut Dollies represented a touch of home in a place where humanity was easily lost.

Providing a welcomed break from K rations, the club cars served donuts well into the summer of 1945. Angela Petesch and the other Doughnut Dollies knew the joy found in serving others though mud and tears.

RED CROSS DONUTS

Ingredients
    1 ½ cups sifted flour
    ¼ teaspoon baking soda
    ¼ teaspoon salt
    ¼ teaspoon butter, melted
    ¼ teaspoon ginger
    ¼ cup molasses
    ¼ cup sour milk
    1 egg, beaten well

Combine half of the flour with the soda, salt and ginger. Combine egg, molasses, sour milk and melted butter. Blend with flour mixture and stir until thoroughly mixed and smooth. Add remaining flour to make dough of sufficient body to be rolled. Roll, on floured board, to thickness of ¼ inch. Cut with donut cutter. Fry in deep fat (360 degrees) until lightly browned, about two to three minutes. Drain on brown paper.

Recipe from *War Through the Hole of a Donut*, page 120
by Angela Petesch, Hunter Halverson Press, 2006

"It isn't enough to talk about peace. One must believe in it. And it isn't enough to believe in it. One must work at it."

Eleanor Roosevelt

Chapter 18

K-Rations

How does a government feed the military?

With K Rations.

The War Department realized that the military needed three daily meals that were nutritious, nonperishable and easy to carry.

The K Ration offered a set of meals that provided each soldier with 3,000 calories and 100 grams of protein. The breakfast unit contained a four-ounce can of chopped ham and egg with opening key, four biscuits, four compressed graham crackers, a two-ounce fruit bar, one packet of water-soluble coffee, sugar, four cigarettes and one piece of gum.

Dinner contained the same, with a few substitutions. For supper soldiers ate a can of beef or pork roast, a two-ounce D Ration, and bouillon powder. All the items fit into a box just under seven inches long, surrounded by an outer box. The day's ration weighed a bit over two pounds.

The chewing gum included conserved water and reduced tension. Some menu substitutions were inevitable as the war continued, but the basic components remained steady—and to some soldiers, monotonous.

Paul McNelis, of the 85th Infantry Division, welcomed the rations during his deployment in Italy. "On the line we survived on K Rations. Mules brought them up the mountains at night along with ammunition and water. We were happy to get them. One good thing was that the box was impregnated with wax. There was just enough that when you set them on fire, it would warm a cup of coffee. A buddy of mine showed me how to make toasted cheese. You open the can, stick your bayonet in it and hold it over the fire to melt the cheese, and then put it on the crackers."[1]

Approximately 550,000 Jews fought in the US armed forces, contributing to the defeat of the Nazis and liberating the camps. Because the Jewish soldiers needed Kosher meals, they would eat the vegetables, crackers, bread, cheese, beans, fruit and other items in the K Ration.

Often, soldiers traded these foods for the ham loaf so that the Kosher eaters could eat with a clear conscience. It was difficult to follow dietary restrictions, but with foraging, bargaining, and ingenuity, the Jewish men stayed healthy and somewhat full.

The lemonade powder provided for the lunch meal was reported as too sour to drink, but worked great as a floor and oven cleaner. Clearly, the K Ration became the meal that the troops loved to hate.

4. The TO, QiC and Camp Mess Officer, will furn nec T, kitchen car facilities, meal tickets, box lunches, and troop train rations, sufficient to cover the number of personnel indicated in par 1 above for length of journey. TDN.

"They fought together as brothers-in-arms. They died together and now they sleep side by side. To them we have a solemn obligation."

Chester W. Nimitz, Admiral of US Navy
Commander in Chief Pacific Ocean

Chapter 19

Sea Cucumbers

During the war, an army nurse needed a make-do attitude to survive nutritionally, especially in Tunisia, North Africa, where the cuisine consisted of hospital rations or local food. First Lieutenant Dorothy Woebbeking chose to forage for that extra tidbit.

In the 10th Field Hospital in Tabarka, Tunisia. Dorothy served with other field nurses in 1943-44 after caring for soldiers across North Africa. They were assigned to the Eleventh Corps, a holding unit for air evacuation and personnel of nearby bases. These nurses trained in field sanitation, mental health, and administration of anesthetics.

Many, like Dorothy, already knew how to scavenge for grub. After all, they rode in the back of Army truck convoys from Casablanca to Tunisia, camping out every night. Some nights, their driver found a way to make them hot meals on the engine of the truck.

The location of the base in Tunisia finally allowed the nurses access to the Mediterranean Sea for some R&R. On one swimming outing, Dorothy made a discovery in one of the water-filled retreats. Explaining a photo of her in a bathing suit she created from parachute scraps, Dorothy wrote: "Sea cucumbers (were) fished out of the Mediterranean last summer while in Africa, at what I think is the best little swimming cove on the whole coast of North Africa."

There is no indication how she prepared the sea cucumbers for consumption, but the bald sea cucumber found in that area of the world can be eaten raw, fried, or pickled. Most often it is added to dishes because it has the ability to soak up flavors of foods and seasonings when cooked.

Often combined with other seafood, soups, or stir-fries, the sea cucumber adds bulk to the dish. These marine creatures need to be soaked in water for twenty-four hours before using.

Like the 59,000 other nurses who provided care to the wounded GIs in field hospitals, hospital ships, trains or planes, Dorothy needed to maintain her health and weight. Sea cucumbers are very low in calories and fat, but high in protein.

Adding protein sources to meals helped keep stomachs feeling full, which made incredibly long nursing shifts more

tolerable. The sea cucumbers also provide antioxidants, B2, niacin, calcium and magnesium.

Sea cucumbers provided a wise choice for army personnel who needed relief from exhaustion, rations and routine. We offer a salute to these amazing women who lived resourcefully in dire situations.

How to Cook Sea Cucumbers

Directions

Cooking sea cucumbers is relatively easy. Rinse the salt off the surface and clean the sand out of the cavity. Soak the cucumbers for two days, changing the water. Then, simply add the marine creature to a large pot of boiling water, cover, and cook for one hour.

If the cucumber is not soft, boil another pot of fresh water and cook until done, testing for softness every 10 to 15 minutes. Cucumbers should bounce back a bit when pressed. Avoid overcooking, or they will fall apart.

Now the sea cucumber is ready to be added to a dish in the same manner that tofu is utilized. This protein can be combined with other seafood, in soups, or stir-fries.

Suggestions by Cleo Lampos

"Attitude is a little thing that makes a big difference."
Winston Churchill

Chapter 20

Nettles:
Foraging for Food

Another meal of field rations and another complaining soldier. Lack of variety and flavor overshadowed the nutrition and energy components of the government-packed food eaten daily by GIs. By 1944, troops were desperate to add variety and bulk to their daily fare. Thank goodness for American ingenuity and the survival experience of many GIs who foraged for food with their families during the Great Depression.

As deployed soldiers scanned the fields of Europe, they recognized stinging nettles growing along the roadsides, in the woods, beside buildings—well, almost everywhere. The greens reach two to four feet tall and have toothed leaves. The trick was to pick the nettles correctly to avoid a rash which was uncomfortable, but not deadly.

The men undoubtedly recalled their days as children foraging with their parents, wearing gloves and long sleeved shirts to prevent being stung. Once the leaves were blanched for five minutes, the greens could be handled safely.

These young soldiers who faced the vicious Normandy battles after D-Day wanted their stomachs to be full, as well as get a boost in energy. The easiest way to achieve that was to make nettle soup. Chopped and boiled in a mess tin or steel helmet, the green mush tasted a bit like Popeye's favorite food, spinach. Ratcheting down the pangs of hunger with tasty greens, the soldiers pressed on with their duty.

Adding nettles to their daily rations proved to be a nutritious choice. Nettles provide vitamins A, C and K as well as minerals. Full of calcium, iron, magnesium, phosphorus, potassium and sodium, the greens were better than a supplemental pill.

In addition, the leaves reduce inflammation, and boost wound healing. Clearly, this provided an added bonus for men in harm's way.

But it wasn't just the GIs who needed nutrition. In 1942, seventy-seven American and Navy nurses were captured by the Japanese while tending injured soldiers in the Philippines. The women spent time in Santo Tomas Internment Camp. After three years of starvation, illness and sacrifice as prisoners of war, all of the women helped each other walk to freedom.

Colonel Nancy Contrell, an historian with the Army Nurse Corps, says, "They were a tough bunch. They had a mission. They were surviving for the boys…and for each other. That does give you a bit of added strength."[2]

The nurses had been recruited specifically by the military from the Dakotas, Maine, Kansas and other states hit hard by the Great Depression. This group of medical trainees spent their childhoods becoming experts at scavenging for food in the wilderness areas near their homes.

They proved to be motivated and capable women in high school, so officials signed them up for overseas duty. Of course, no one expected they would become POWs.

The *Angels of Bataan*, as the captured nurses were called, survived by eating roots, flowers, slugs, and weeds. This list of weeds in the Philippines includes a locally grown variety of nettles which grows in abundance. The fact that these women endured their incarceration with no formal survival training stands as a tribute to their inner strength and their early years of deprivation. The nurses knew that survival depended on hunkering around each other and sharing what little they had with the weakest, even their nettle soup.

Audrey Hepburn and the Dutch people suffered terribly during the war, especially in the winter of 1944-45, when starvation claimed many Hollander lives. Audrey "survived by eating nettles and tulip bulbs and drinking water to fill her stomach...She had jaundice and edema. She suffered from anemia the rest of her life...She was the same age as Ann Frank and said, 'That was the girl who didn't make it, and I did.' Her voice would crack and her eyes would fill with tears."[3]

Those English who endured food rationing went into the verges and hedgerows in early spring to forage nettles. These greens had already been a mainstay in the diet as Britain's "oldest pudding," dating back to 6,000 B.C.

Creative chefs used the blanched leaves as spinach in pasta or an omelete, and for many, teatime included nettle tea. During the Blitz and the ensuing rocket attacks, Britain's hungry population devised many variations in recipes to include the nutrition of nettles.

Knowing how to forage for nettles provided the needed bulk and nutrients needed by soldiers, nurses and those living in war zones. Hopefully, the younger generations will learn some of these skills.

HOW TO COOK NETTLES

Cut off the upper leaves of the nettle plant, no larger than 3 inches wide.

Separate the leaves from the stalk and put the leaves in warm water for 10 minutes.

Blanch the nettles in boiling water with a pinch of salt for five minutes.

Add the cooked nettles to an egg omelet, or with rice. Makes a tasty soup.

Nettle Soup

Ingredients
  ½ pound stinging nettles
  1 onion
  2 tablespoons unsalted butter
  1 teaspoon sea salt
  1 pound potatoes
  6 cups chicken or vegetable broth
  ½ teaspoon black pepper
  ¼ teaspoon nutmeg
  Optional: ½ cup cream, sour cream, yogurt or horseradish cream

Rinse the nettles under cold running water. Wear gloves
Peel and chop onion.

Melt 1 tablespoon of butter in large pot. Add onion and salt. Cook 3 minutes.

Add chopped potatoes and broth to the onions. Boil, then simmer 15 minutes.

Add nettles and simmer 10 minutes. Add remaining butter, pepper and nutmeg.

Puree soup with immersion blender.

Stir in cream or other options.

Serve soup hot, garnished with sour cream, yogurt of horse-radish cream.[4]

"It's not enough that we do our best; sometimes we have to do what's required."
Winston Churchill

European Challenges

Chapter 21

How Tulips
Helped the Dutch Survive

The Dutch who survived the starving years of WWII use two quotes when speaking about eating tulip bulbs.

"They taste like a slap in the face."

That says it all as far as most Hollanders are concerned.

J.H. Warmerdam grew up in the Netherlands during the famine winter of 1944-45. He recalls that the tulip bulbs gave skin rashes to the people, possibly from an allergic reaction. He concedes that they were not a tasty meal. The entire population of the country agrees that the petals are somewhat edible, but not the bulbs. Most Hollanders described the tulip bulbs as tasting bitter and dry.

Father Leo Zonneveld recalls. "Even though much of Western Europe had been liberated from Nazi control, Holland remained under their firm grip. I remember the hunger. We were forced to eat tulip bulbs and sugar beets because there was no other food." He would not agree to the saying, "Hunger sweetens even raw beans." Instead he maintains, "Bread made from tulips is not very good; I can tell you that!"

Zonneveld continues. "The skin of the bulb is removed, pretty much like an onion, and so is the center, because that is poisonous. Then it is dried and baked in the oven. My mother or older sisters would grind the bulbs to a meal-like consistency. Then they would mix the meal with water and salt, shape it like a meatloaf and bake it. I can still remember the taste of it: like we eat sawdust."[1]

During the winter of 1944-45, food and fuel stocks became exhausted as the harsh weather took a death toll on Dutch citizens who starved or froze to death. Due to the war, tulip growers had not planted bulbs earlier in the spring, and decided to take their old dry tulip bulbs to the grocery stores to sell as food.

One tulip grower claimed to have sold 2500 tons of bulbs: "Crocuses for coffee, daffodils and hyacinths for fodder, and tulips for the humans."[2]

The government assured the Hollanders that the tulip bulbs were rich in carbohydrates and could be used as a surrogate for potatoes. One four-ounce portion of tulip bulbs contained 148 calories, 3 grams of protein and 32 grams of carbohydrates. Many citizens survived on 500-600 calories per day.

The Food Agency in The Hague published a folder in

January, 1945. It contained recipes designed for tulip bulbs. In addition to tulip bulb soup, other culinary creations included porridge, mashed tulip bulbs, vegetables and tulip bulbs, fried and roasted bulbs, and sweet tulip bulb cookies. Two methods for making flour and keeping it useable were included—very informative and useful suggestions.

The Monkman Family resorted to the tulip solution. Susan Monkman recalls: "The tulip bulbs were unbelievably sharp-edged. No amount of simmering would soften them. Nevertheless we were happy to chew them slowly and carefully. They left us with sore throats for days." The throat irritation was reduced if a few carrots or a sugar beet was mixed with the bulbs.

At the end of the war, teenager Audrey Hepburn stood five feet six inches tall, but only weighed eighty-eight pounds. "We ate nettles and everyone tried to boil grass—in addition to the tulip bulbs—but I really couldn't stand it."[3]

Over 10,000 civilians died of malnutrition that winter. How many more people lived on the edge of starvation is anyone's guess. Which explains the second quote that Dutch survivors of eating tulips quip to their children.

"Je hebt geen honger, je hebt trek." Translated, it means: "You are not hungry, you only have appetite."[4]

For the Dutch, real hunger means that a person is ready to eat anything they can acquire, including old, dry tulip bulbs. The bulbs sustained many during the winter of famine, and embedded an appreciation for food in the Hollanders.

So, the old timers pass along two worthy quotes to the next generation when speaking of eating tulips.

"They taste like a slap in the face."

"You are not hungry, you only have appetite."

RECIPE FOR PREPARING BULBS
From the Amsterdam Tulip Museum

Remove the brown skin and cut off the remnants of the roots.

Cut the bulb in half from top to bottom, remove flower stem.

Wash thoroughly to clear remaining soil.

Cook for roughly thirty minutes, similar to potatoes.[4]

DR. MEES' TULIP SOUP

Ingredients
　One liter of water
　1 onion
　4-6 tulip bulbs
　Seasoning, salt, teaspoon of oil, curry

Cut up the onion and brown with the oil and curry.
Add water and seasoning, bring to boil while grating the cleaned bulbs into the boiling liquid.'
　Salt to taste.

Dr. Mees claims the soup has no nutritional value, but fills the stomach. However, too much tulip consumption causes indigestion.

"The measure of a life, after all, is not its duration, but its donation."

Corrie Ten Boom
Dutch Resistor and concentration camp survivor

Chapter 22

Resourceful Eating

The Third Reich gripped France in its march to Britain. The Channel Islands were no match for their forces, so the Germans invaded and occupied these islands during the war. One of the Channel Islands, Guernsey, became the only British territory that the Germans controlled.

Many of the island's children had been sent to the safety of the British mainland, some with their parents. But the rest fell under the control of new German overseers, who took over with no resistance. This action immediately cut off Guernsey citizens from the rest of the world.

The Nazis brought in thousands of foreign prisoners to construct concrete bunkers, gun emplacements and tunnels for future use against the Brits. The prisoners were treated as slaves and given little to eat.

The island received no mainland supplies. Food sources were only what the farmers grew or foraged, so the islanders planted potatoes. The Germans confiscated most farm animals for their own consumption, and persons hiding produce or edible animals endured severe punishment.

By the winter of 1944, both Guernsey residents and soldiers survived on starvation rations. The Swedish ship SS Vega, chartered by the International Red Cross, brought in food which saved many from death. Soon, the war came to an end and the island was liberated. Supplies sailed from Great Britain until the island's agriculture, animals, and poultry farms were re-established.

During the Nazi occupation, Guernsey cooks made *potato peel pie* from meager ingredients. This pie represents the formidable spirit of the Guernsey people surviving under oppressive conditions. Using the peels of potatoes for a topping emphasizes the dire straits of these island citizens. Thus, the dish symbolizes the will to resist and live.

The classic *potato peel pie* consists of mashed potatoes, peels for the crust, perhaps a beet, and a bit of milk for flavoring. The peels are either criss-crossed across the top or laid over the potato filling  as a crust. The baking crisps the peelings.

This updated recipe for Potato Peel Pie has been developed by Erin Odom, who suggests that the dish be served at a book club, as a staple for a family breakfast, or a brunch.

POTATO PEEL PIE

Ingredients
    30 ounces total hash browns (frozen)
    2 cups half and half
    ¼ cup butter
    ¼ cup diced onions
    Salt, pepper and garlic to taste.
    ¼ cup parmesan cheese

Method
    Preheat oven to 400 degrees F.
    Spread hash browns in the bottom of a greased 9-inch pie plate to make a crust.
    Bake crust 15-20 minutes. Reduce heat to 350 degrees F.
    Make the pie filling by combining the rest of the hash browns, half and half, butter, onions and seasonings in a saucepan. Stir until butter is melted and everything is well combined.
    Spread filling on top of pie crust.
    Sprinkle the top of the pie with parmesan cheese.
    Bake for 1 hour on 350 degrees F, or until top is fully browned.
                                              Recipe courtesy of
    https://thehumbledhomemaker.com/potato-peel-pie-recipe/

Suggestion
    Procure a potato. Wash it thoroughly. Peel the skin and set aside. Finely dice the potato and incorporate the pieces into the pie filling. Just before placing the pie into the oven, position the peels on the top. These will serve as a reminder of the sacrifices of the Guernsey people during the war, and the debt of gratitude that we owe to those who have gone before us.

"Hardships often prepare ordinary people for an extraordinary destiny."
C. S. Lewis

Chapter 23

The Land Girls

The young professionals who enlisted in the Women's Land Army did not pack their evening dresses with coordinated heels. As farm workers, their attire needed to be practical. Clothed in a uniform of brown corduroy, brown brogues, fawn knee-length woolen socks, a green V-neck pullover, a fawn shirt and a brown cowboy style hat, their distinct attire made a bold statement.

Their country's food was at stake, and these women had traded their stylish flair for functionality on the farm. They made this personal sacrifice for the war effort.

Iris Walters spoke for so many. "The girls came from all walks of life and various parts of the country. We had some from Yorkshire and London. It must have been quite a culture shock for them. I, having been born in the country, didn't feel quite so bad."[1]

The Land Girls comprised the Women's Land Army, which helped to provide Britain with food when German U-boats were destroying merchant ships bringing supplies from America. With a dependence on imported food, the country faced severe rationing, malnutrition, and possible starvation. With so many young men called into the armed forces, the older farmers who were left behind needed people to harvest and plant crops. To respond to this need, the government resurrected the WLA, which had performed this service during WW1.

In December 1941, the government passed the National Service Act, allowing conscription of women into the armed forces for vital war work. At first, only single women between twenty and thirty and widows without children were called up, but the age limit expanded to include 19 to 43 year olds.

The choices for women included the armed forces, farming, and industry. By 1943, 80,000 women enlisted in the Land Army as Land Girls.

The WLA fell under the control of the Ministry of Agriculture with Lady Denman as the head of the agency. Lady Denman stated: "The land army fights in the fields. It is in the fields of Britain that the most critical battle of the present war may be fought and won." As a leading figure in the Women's Institute movement, she was also interested in rural affairs. Lady Denman expected that the Land Girls would be treated well as they worked alongside others with whom they would develop lifelong friendships.

These women were trained "on the job" to accomplish a wide range of agricultural tasks. They milked cows, delivered lambs, managed poultry, plowed fields, and harvested crops. Catching rats and digging ditches also made the list. Some six thousand women worked in the Timber Corps, chopping down trees and running sawmills.

The Land Girls worked fifty hours a week or more, especially in the summer when crops were growing and animals needed extra

A woman and her daughter model the W.L.A.A. uniforms adopted during World War I and later, World War II. (Photo courtesy the National Archives)

care. They endured cold and rain. Fortunately, they lived on the farms where they worked, or slept in hostels.

But many were homesick and longed for weekends to visit back home. Others enjoyed the freedom from the bombing raids over London. The farmers paid them a salary, but it was difficult to ensure everyone was compensated at the same rate.

A farmer from Northamptonshire wrote in praise of Land Girl Mary Hall: "I cannot speak too highly of her, as it has been no easy task for a girl to go through the wet and cold we have had this winter…She has never missed a day or been late all through the severe weather we have had…I am afraid I have had thought of land girls as summertime workers, but Mary has proved to me that I am wrong."[3]

The WLA badge depicted a wheat sheaf as a symbol of the Land Girls' agricultural work. The organization had an official magazine, *The Land Girl*, which boosted morale, and their special song banded them together.

Back to the Land, we must all lend a hand.
To the farms and the fields we must go.
There's a job to be done, Though we can't fire a gun.
We can still do our bit with the hoe.[2]

The women of Great Britain donned the uniform needed for farming and helped keep the nation's supply of food adequate for the duration of the war. With spades in hand, the Land Women labored for their country and the men who were defending its shores. Their selfless work made the difference.

Grandma Abson lived through WWII in England. The campaign to "win the war on the kitchen front" was about using food wisely and maximizing gluts of produce in season. This is Grandma Abson's Rhubarb Crumble recipe, dedicated to the memory of the Land Girls who cut cabbages out in the field in freezing weather.

RHUBARB CRUMBLE

By Grandma Abson and Meryl White
(Used with permission)

Ingredients
  6-8 sticks of rhubarb
  2 oz of soft brown sugar
  1tsp ginger

Wash and cut rhubarb sticks into chunks. Place on a baking tray and sprinkle sugar over them. Then cook in 325 degrees F for 15 minutes until tender. Remove from the oven, place in a deep pie dish and sprinkle ginger on top of the rhubarb.

For the Crumble
  4 oz plain flour
  4 oz porridge oats (or rolled oats)
  4 oz butter
  2 oz demerara sugar (or light brown sugar)

Turn up the oven to 350 degrees. Stir butter into flour until it resembles breadcrumbs. Add the porridge oats and sugar. Spread the crumble mixture over the rhubarb and bake for 30-35 minutes until golden. Remove from the oven and let cool for 10 minutes before serving.

More WWII recipes can be found in the e-book, *Grandma Abson's Traditional Baking,* by Meryl White, who believes the secret of the Rhubarb Crumble is the addition of ginger.

"The land army fights in the fields. It is in the fields of Britain that the most critical battle of the present war may well be fought and won."
Lady Denman
Director of the Land Girls

Chapter 24

Dig for Victory

Food can be an effective weapon against an enemy. As German submarines stalked supply ships to England, the British population began to feel the shortage of imported food. Rationing began in January, 1940, and as an island country, Great Britain now depended upon fifty million tons of imported produce.

By 1941, that amount of available food was cut in two by the success of the German subs. The slogan, "Spades not ships!" motivated people to start cultivating any patch of soil around them to become self-sufficient from imports.

Open spaces were transformed into garden allotments for those who lived in apartments. Public parks were cultivated and planted with vegetables. The lawns outside of the Tower of London eschewed their usual flower display for edible plants.

Even the Oxford College lawns were turned over for planting. With spades in hand, the population began to *Dig for Victory*. By 1943, over 3.5 million allotments produced over a million tons of vegetables.

Betty Hall of Lewisham remembered her parents were given an allotment in Ladywell Park on a plot which had previously been popular with picnickers.

"Consequently when my father dug over the plot, he found quite a hoard of pennies and ha'pennies. He bought his first lot of seeds with the cash."[1]

The ingenuity of the British people helped them to grow food in unlikely places. Wolsey Motor employees in Birmingham were allotted growing spaces, and the workers used scrap car windscreens to make cloches. These transparent covers were placed over new growing plants to protect them from the elements until the plants were hardy. This strategy helped to grow produce all year long by extending the growing season.

"To everything there is a season." The government printed plans for growing a harvest all year round. Most gardeners planted potatoes, peas, pole and bush beans, carrots, parsnips, onions, shallots, marrows, celery, lettuce, radishes, tomatoes, cabbage, cauliflower, spinach, and Brussel sprouts. Frank, whose parents had an allotment in London, claims: "The sprouts, like the parsnips, were 'best' when there'd been a 'bit of a frost.'"[2]

Government leaflets also instructed the new gardeners

on using tool sheds, seedbed planting and composting. One suggestion was to build walls in a square and fill this area with soil. This strategy allowed for deep rooting food plants to be put in tight places. These raised beds made growing manageable.

The government also

introduced companion planting, putting different plants in the same bed. By having a variety in a raised bed, different pests and diseases are attracted and can be repelled by the other plants

Fruit bushes yielded black and red berries, black and red currants, gooseberries, rhubarb, and strawberries. Apple trees produced enough for bartering with neighbors. All fruit that could not be eaten immediately was made into jams and mild wines. Nothing was wasted.

Even the Royal Family joined the nation to *Dig for Victory*. Fourteen-year-old Princess Elizabeth and her sister Princess Margaret joined the rest of wartime Britain in producing food. The Windsor Castle garden brought fresh vegetables to the table while the Princesses enjoyed the art of planting and harvesting.

By 1943, over fifty-five per-cent of household were growing fresh organic fruits and vegetables in community plots or spaces around their homes. In addition to getting their fingers into the soil, the British were encouraged to keep chickens, rabbits and goats. Droppings from these animals were used to compost the gardens.

Pigs became popular, as they could feed on kitchen scraps.

"Pig Clubs" were started for collecting food leftovers in big bins to feed the animals. Becoming self-sufficient employed the time and energy of the nation.

The Germans tried to make food a weapon against the British, but the pluck and energy of a people determined to live free foiled that plan. As the Brits spaded in their lawns, they did more than *Dig for Victory*. They saved their civilization.

With rationing and the production of myriads of vegetables, new recipes had to be created. Woolton Pie was developed by the Chef of the Savoy Hotel and named after Lord Woolton, head of the Ministry of Food. This is one variation of that recipe.

WOOLTON PIE

Ingredients
    1 lb. cut potatoes
    1 lb. cauliflower
    1 lb. sliced carrots
    1 lb. spinach
    3 onions chopped
    1 tablespoon oatmeal
    Salt, pepper, oregano to taste
    Chopped parsley

Method

Place all the vegetables and ingredients into a pot.

Add enough water to cover. Keep stirring the mixture until thickened.

Let the vegetables cool before placing in a deep pie dish.

Sprinkle with parsley.

Cover the top with a rolled-out pie crust.

Bake at 350 degrees F until crust is golden brown.

Serve with a side of hot brown gravy.

"Let 'Dig for Victory' be the motto of everyone with a garden and of every able-bodied man and woman capable of digging an allotment in their spare time."
Radio Broadcast, Oct. 3, 1939

Conclusion

Words that launched The Greatest Generation

Through the corridors of time, the words that challenged and inspired a nation at war to action still speak to the present generation.

> *"Every gun that is made, every warship launched, every rocket fired, signifies in the final sense a theft from those who hunger and are not fed, those who are cold and are not clothed."*
> Dwight D. Eisenhower

> *"This generation of Americans has a rendezvous with destiny."*
> Franklin D. Roosevelt

> *"You must do the things you think you cannot do."*
> Eleanor Roosevelt

> *"America was not built on fear. America was built on courage, on imagination and an unbeatable determination to do the job at hand."*
> Harry S. Truman

Conclusion

"It is wonderful what great strides can be made when there is a resolute purpose behind them."
Sir Winston Churchill

"Courage is fear holding on a minute longer."
George S. Patton

"Duty, honor, country. Those three hallowed words reverently dictate what you ought to be, what you can be, what you will be."
Douglas MacArthur

"How wonderful it is that nobody need wait a single moment before starting to improve the world."
Anne Frank

The common folks of the world have left a legacy of sacrifice and perseverance that is unparalleled. The men who left home and country to fight on foreign shores. The women who stood in the gap as Land Girls, victory gardeners, Rosie the Riveter, and military support. The children who helped in scrap metal drives, paper round-ups, and in canning the produce from millions of gardens. These ordinary people hunkered together to defeat a formidable enemy. Their legacy is spoken in three words.

They are: The Greatest Generation.

Photo Credits & References

Chapter 1

https://unwritten-record.blogs.archives.gov/2014/08/12/
supporting-troops-on-the-homefront-the-north-platte-nebraska-canteen/

https://commons.wikimedia.org/wiki/File:Alex_Gurney-(1944a).jpeg

Chicken Soup for the Veteran's Soul, edited by Jack Canfield, Mark Victory Hansen, and Sidney R. Slager, Health Communications, Inc. Deerfield Beach, Florida, 2001, page 172.

Once Upon a Town, by Bob Green, Perennial, an imprint of Harper Collin Publisher, New York City, 2002, page 177.

Once Upon a Town, by Bob Green, page 48.

Chapter 2

https://commons.wikimedia.org/wiki/File:1920_Jell-O_Cookbook.jpg

"A Social History of Jell-O Salad: The Rise and Fall of an American Icon," by Sarah Grey. www.Serious Eats/culture/food history

Chapter 3

https://commons.wikimedia.org/wiki/File:Hormel_Luncheon_Loaf,_
SPAM_Museum,_Austin_MN_(34179390752).jpg

1.*Soldiering On: Spam and World War II*, By Brenda Junkin: Plain Dealer Reporter, March 29, 2019.

2. *America in WWII*, by Bruce Haydt, June issue, 206 , for National WWII Museum, New Orleans.

3. Haydt, Bruce

Chapter 4

Photo Credits & References

https://pixabay.com/photos/potatoes-vegetables-erdfrucht-bio-1585075/

https://commons.wikimedia.org/wiki/File:I%27m_a_Protective_Food_-_Says_Potato_Pete_Art.IWMPST20603.jpg

https://commons.wikimedia.org/wiki/File:I_Make_a_Good_Soup_-_Says_Potato_Pete_Art.IWMPST6080.jpg

"Potato Pete", *The Home Front Housewife*. Blogspot.com/2015/02.

"The 1940's Experiment: Cooking up Wartime Recipes to Save Money and Lose 100 Pounds in Weight," by Carolyn Ekins, December 6, 2009 online.

Chapter 5

https://pixabay.com/photos/eat-dine-mashed-potatoes-liver-180826/

"Changing Eating Habits on the Home Front: Lost Lessons from World War II Research," by Brian Wansink, professor of consumer behavior at Cornell University, 2002 paper

"Here's the Scoop on Eleanor Roosevelt's Notoriously Bad White House Meals", by Kelsey Rae Dimberg for Taste of Home online.

Patriotic Food Show: Official Recipe Book containing all demonstrations given during the Patriotic Food Show. Women's Central Committee on Food Conservation, St. Louis Missouri, February 2-10, 1918, page 8.

https://www.newyorker.com/magazine/2010/11/22/the-first-kitchen

Chapter 6

https://atascaderonews.com/news/local-news/local-veteran-shares-memories-of-wwii/

Chapter 7

Adapted from https://www.nationalgeographic.com/culture/food/theplate/2014/08/13/thebutter-wars-when-margarine-was-pink/

Chapter 8

https://www.archives.gov/

https://www.flickr.com/photos/35740357@N03/4545457453/ (The U.S. National Archives)

https://content.libraries.wsu.edu/digital/collection/propaganda/id/188/

https://en.wikipedia.org/wiki/C-ration#/media/File:C_Ration_B_unit_
(1941)_with_contents.jpg

Chapter 9

https://digital.library.unt.edu/ark:/67531/metadc544/m1/1/

"Kelly Holthus on Victory Gardens," an interview for livinghistoryfarm.org/
farminginthe40s/movies/holthus-crops.

Kelly Holthus worked in rural banks, becoming President of Cornerstone
Bank in York.

Chapter 10

https://pixabay.com/photos/pickles-billet-cucumbers-1799731/

https://pixabay.com/photos/vegetables-vegetarian-tomatoes-food-3386212/

Chapter 11

https://commons.wikimedia.org/wiki/File:Elaine_Norwich,_WLA_
(Women%27s_Land_Army)_girl_from_Fall_River,_Massachusettes,_
showing_bushel_of_beans_she_has_just..._-_NARA_-_512803.tif

https://www.archives.gov/publications/prologue/1993/winter/landarmy.
html

"The Nation's Crops Need You", p.187, and Women's Land Army, Extension
Farm Labor Program, pp.15.

Women's Land Army, Extension Farm Labor Program, page 6.

Samuel I. Rosenman, ed.; The Public Papers and Addresses of Franklin D.
Roosevelt (1938-1950), vol. 12, The Tide Turns, 1943, pp. 34-35.

Records Concerning the Farm Labor Program, General and Other Corre-
spondance and Related Records, 1943-48, box 8, Publicity, Records of the
Extension Service, Record Group 33, National Archives, Washington, DC.

Chapter 12

Photo credit: Leone Dunkelberg

Chapter 13

Chapter 14

https://commons.wikimedia.org/wiki/File:Plain_Chocolate_2oz._Military_rations,_World_War_II.JPG (Nederlands: Plain Chocolate 2oz. Military rations, World War II Photographed in the collection of the National Liberation Museum 1944-1945)

Chapter 15

https://commons.wikimedia.org/wiki/File:Hershey_Tropical_Bar_SI.jpg

Chapter 16

Chapter 17

https://commons.wikimedia.org/wiki/File:Red_Cross_girls_carrying_fresh_doughnuts_from_an_improvised_kitchen,_Constantine,_Algeria,_1943_(27503466272).jpg

https://commons.wikimedia.org/wiki/File:Lot-11580-2_(27602872005).jpg

Chapter 18

"The World's Best Fed Army," by Richard Beranty, warfarehistorynetwork.com/2016/09/30/

Chapter 20

1. "5 Survival Foods Made By Soldiers During WW2 On the Normandy Front" by Fergus Mason, October 29, 2018, Ask a Prepper How to… online.

2. "The Angles of Bataan: The World War II Nurses Who Survived Three Years in a Japanese Prison Camp," by Katherine, Posted on May 12, 2019

3. "Audrey Hepburn nearly starved to death during World War II", by Stephanie Nolasco, September 26, 2017, Fox News.com

4. "Stinging Nettles Soup", By Molly Watson, 1122/19, The Spruce Eats online.

https://en.wikipedia.org/wiki/File:Audrey_Hepburn_1956.jpg

Chapter 21

Father Leo Zonneveld wrote his remarks for the Veterans History Project online.

"Tulips," by Deane in Greens/Pot Herb, Plants. Website: Eat the Weeds and other things, too.

"Audrey Hepburn Weighed 88 lbs After WWII, Son Reveals," by Liz McNeil, People Magazine, June23, 2015.

"Eating tulip bulbs", by FLUWEL, a tulip bulb provider online.

"Eating Tulip Bulbs During WWII" Amsterdam Tulip Museum, September 25, 2017

https://pixabay.com/photos/flower-bulbs-tulips-garden-plant-2853524/

Chapter 22

https://pixabay.com/photos/casserole-potato-casserole-eat-227997/

Chapter 23

grandmaabson.blogspot.com/2013/02/land-girls-provide-women-power. html

https://www.archives.gov/publications/prologue/1993/winter/landarmy.html

https://unsplash.com/photos/bplZQxsEbdo

"The Women's Land Army," by C N Trueman, historylearningsite.co.uk The History Learning Site, 20 April 2915, 18 Dec. 2019.

"Women's Land Army" Fact File, June 1939-1950. WW2 People's War, and archive of World War Two memories, written by the public, gathered by BBC bbc.co.uk/history.ww2peopleswar/timeline/factfiles

The Taste of War: World War II and the Battle for Food, By Lizzie Collingham, The Penguin Press, New York, 2012 Chapter 5

Chapter 24

https://commons.wikimedia.org/wiki/File:Dig_for_Victory_Art. IWMPST0696.jpg

https://commons.wikimedia.org/wiki/File:Village_Gardens_Feed_School-children-_Food_Production_at_Knighton-on-teme,_Worcestershire,_ England,_UK,_1943_D17504.jpg

Photo Credits & References

https://commons.wikimedia.org/wiki/File:%22Night_sight_can_mean_life_of_dealth._Eat_carrots_and_leafly_greens_or_yellow_vegetables,_rich_in_vitamins%22_-_NARA_-_515071.jpg

https://commons.wikimedia.org/wiki/File:Your_Own_Vegetables_All_the_Year_Round_-_If_You_Dig_For_Victory_Now_Art.IWMPST17009.jpg

https://commons.wikimedia.org/wiki/File:Allotments_in_Kensington_Gardens,_London,_all_part_of_the_%27Dig_for_Victory%27_scheme_in_1942._D8336.jpg

1. "Dig for Victory campaign is in danger of being forgotten", by Helena Horton, January 10, 2019, telegraph.co.uk online.

2. "The Allotment," by Sharoncitizen, for WW2 People's War, An archive of World War Two Memories, written by the public, gathered by the BBC. Bbc.co.uk/history/ww2peoples war/stories

Additional Photo Credits

About the Author

Words have always been comfort food for Gail Kittleson. After instructing expository writing and English as a Second Language, she began writing seriously. Intrigued by the World War II era, Gail creates women's historical fiction from her northern Iowa home and also facilitates writing workshops/retreats.

She and her husband, a retired Army chaplain, enjoy their grandchildren and in winter, Arizona's Mogollon Rim Country. You can count on Gail's heroines to ask honest questions, act with integrity, grow in faith, and face hardships with spunk.

Visit Gail online at: GailKittleson.com

About the Author

For 26 years, Cleo Lampos used storytelling, biography and history to reach her classrooms of students in the public schools. Currently, she employs the same techniques to mesmerize senior citizens in community college extension classes.

With a Bachelor's Degree in Education from University of Wisconsin-Whitewater and Master's Degree in Special Education from St. Xavier University-Chicago, Lampos has written seven books and numerous magazine articles. She lives in the Chicago, Illinois area where she quilts, joins her husband in urban gardening, and enjoys her eleven grandchildren.

Visit Cleo online at: CleoLampos.com

Also Available From

WordCrafts Press

All My Goodbyes
  by Jan Cline

Before History Dies
  by Jacob Carter

Saturday & the Witch Woman
  by Dr. Thomas O. Ott

The Rose and the Whip
  by Jae Hodges

Angela's Treasures
  by Marian Rizzo

www.wordcrafts.net